SUCCESSFUL
BUSINESS
THINKING

SUCCESSFUL
BUSINESS
THINKING

THE BUSINESS PHILOSOPHY OF
A. M. SULLIVAN

Foreword by Peter F. Drucker

Dun & Bradstreet

BUSINESS LIBRARY

LONDON
W. FOULSHAM & CO., LTD.
NEW YORK   TORONTO   CAPE TOWN   SYDNEY

W. FOULSHAM & CO. LTD.

Yeovil Road, Slough, Bucks., England

ISBN 0 572 00747 7 ✓

Printed in Great Britain by
Bristol Typesetting Co. Ltd., Barton Manor, Bristol

658.01

CONTENTS

FOREWORD

Part of A. M. Sullivan's magic as a business writer lies in his being exceedingly knowledgeable about business and deeply interested in it. He knows the reality of the big organization first-hand, having been for many years himself an executive in a large and growing concern. He knows how business is conducted, how executives think and work, and what really matters to them, their associates, and their company. He knows that business is not only abstract laws and economic forces, but, above all, people striving for accomplishment. There is compassion in his view of business and the businessman, but also shrewdness. He knows " what fools these mortals be ". But he also knows how hard they strive. Everyone reading this book will be struck by its practicality.

At first reading, A. M. Sullivan sounds almost too simple. No big words, no complex sentences, no portentious announcements or " sensational breakthroughs ". One seemingly obvious thought is put down in a quiet, well-modulated voice and in a few beautifully scanning sentences. Every essay seems almost gossamer-light. But somehow the few quiet sentences stay with the reader. He finds himself going back to them and reading them again and again.

What Sullivan says may be obvious indeed. But it is also challenging, probing, questioning, stimulating. These fragile threads of thought, the reader comes to realize, have the strength of pure crystal. And they can carry almost any load of thought and reflection. Above all, these apparently general, and sometimes abstract, comments have an uncanny habit of becoming concrete all of a sudden, and pertinent to what the businessman does or what he considers doing.

He says exactly what he means and means exactly what he says. No one writing in the field of business, can match the unity of thought and word, of medium and message that characterizes even the most casual of the chapters in this volume.

Shrewd and practical, but convinced, at the same time, that values matter and that expedient decisions are wrong decisions and will not work; dedicated to business as a major human sphere and as a mighty servant of man, yet fully conscious of the difficulties the businessman faces every day as he goes about his tasks.

Anyone who reads this book will learn a great deal about business. But he will also learn a great deal about himself. For in every chapter, Sullivan asks the reader " What manner of man are you? What manner of man do you want to be?" It is not that Sullivan is " critical " of business as the term is commonly understood. He believes in it fully. But because he believes in business, he demands and expects much from the businessman.

Peter F. Drucker

PART I

The Man In Management

The Man In Management

Understanding the individual is probably the most challenging aspect of successful management, whether in business, education or government. Averages are useful in group psychology, because human behaviour *en masse* is measurable by a statistical gauge. The individual, however, is always a tantalizing enigma because of his perverse refusal to conform to any rigid rule or measure of intellect, emotion, or attitude. What creates loyalty, affection, integrity, reticence in one man creates suspicion, selfishness, dishonesty in another. It is the elusive and intangible factors that make human relations fascinating.

One of the most important qualities of the good manager of people is an emotional sensitivity that goes beyond mere rational judgement. The leader who exudes confidence, sympathy, and candour tends to evoke the same qualities in the people around him. The chill, appraising eye that betrays a bloodless, calculating mental machine can create uncertainty, self-consciousness, and a sense of inferiority.

Good management is not only the gift of identifying talent, but the art of recognition of strength and weakness, and the proper encouragement of the best in subordinates.

The world of physics and chemistry has complex equations. In mathematics, the Arab who invented zero revolutionized computation and freed it from the strictures of Roman numerals. Hamilton, by inventing the quaternions, enlarged the scope of calculus for the modern mathematician. Einstein, who upset Newtonian mechanics, opened a new universe for speculative science.

But the human equation is still the old enigma, and despite our progress in the study of behaviour, the human mind is the area of most promising and rewarding adventure. As Alexander Pope said in his rhymed essay, " The proper study of mankind is man "—and *man* is still the most engaging syllable in management.

Managing One's Self

One of the first lessons a child learns is that he cannot run away from his shadow, and a second is that he cannot act independently of his reflection in the mirror. These lessons have to be re-learned frequently in our mature years, because no man can evade the aura of identity and personality which surrounds him.

" Be yourself " is sound advice as far as it goes, since in trying to be " somebody else " we usually suffer failure as an imitation. The organization man who tries to be an executive composite ends up as a nobody. The art of enlarging one's personality comes from inner effort rather than exterior polish—from a mental and spiritual growth rather than acquired mannerisms affecting speech or attitudes.

Blessed is he who can relax among his superiors as well as inferiors and be respectful to both. A relaxed personality invites other people to drop the mask and identify themselves.

The extrovert with his braying laughter, punishing handshake and positive opinions does not need to lie with his tongue; everything about him points to a false set of values and frequently to an insecure person. The introvert is often a liar to himself, because of self-pity, the illusion of persecution, and blindness to personal faults. He is prone to envy and is apt to sneer at and belittle the success of others.

" Be yourself " takes on greater significance when it is identified with the old Greek adage " Know thyself." Self-knowledge is the result of a candid and sometimes painful appraisal of personal qualities, a discipline which, through recognition, often converts inherent weaknesses to strengths.

In business, where a man is privileged to succeed or fail according to his abilities, the greatest obstacle to progress is the temptation to blame difficulties on other people. The man who is operating a losing business can be helped by good advice, but it is a tragic fact that the entrepreneur who needs help the most will not confess to emotional faults or errors in judgement. He will point to inventory problems, poor merchandising techniques, wrong neighbourhood appraisal and other evidence of the ineptitude of others.

The selfish executive is loath to delegate until his plans go awry. Then the repair job is dumped into the lap of some middle-management man who is expected to be a face saver as well as a trouble shooter. No executive can catch all the bouquets and duck all the brickbats indefinitely, nor can he ride the momentum of an uphill trend without eventually bucking the drag of gravity.

To be yourself, and to know yourself calls for a daily review of conduct under the tensions of business and social life. One cannot exist without tensions. They test the mettle of our will and the stamina of our character. We cannot evade the anxiety that tension creates when we face necessary decisions. We cannot avoid exposure to a host of eyes waiting to measure the quality of our judgement.

No man can be right all the time, but he *can* be himself. He can act as a thinking individual, willing to risk his own reputation before risking someone elses. Managing one's self should be a primary exercise in personal ethics.

Profile Of A Managing Director

The successful managing director is identified by these qualities, talents, and eccentricities:

1. He leads by example more than directive, and those who follow feel the pull of his personality rather than the push of his will power.
2. He surrounds himself with experts but often confounds them by his ability to clarify and simplify, to get at essentials.
3. He has the curved vision of the prophet who can see the goal ahead without disturbing too many who stand in the light.
4. He hates technical jargon and under the pretence of ignorance gets information reduced to language any executive understands.
5. He listens with respect to at least one management maverick who disturbs the economic pattern makers with off-beat ideas and auguries.
6. He is logical up to the point of decision, when he may upset the obvious with inspired judgement—the hidden gift of leadership.
7. He is a planner who describes perimeters of time and space, leaving the inner dimensions to the man at the drafting board.

8.   He has an imaginative approach toward opportunities for growth, preferring a slightly larger measure of risk than caution.

9.   He has an eye for detail but no love of it, leaving that chore for the near-sighted and the pencil-chewers.

10.   He picks " yes " men who see potentials beyond the question asked, and " no " men who are specialists in methods, techniques, and cost accounting.

11.   He has more respect for the man who makes a wrong decision in an emergency than for the man who wrings his hands and takes refuge in the rule book.

12.   He wants the facts in black and white but is well aware that every observer colours his report according to his circumstances and interests.

13.   He likes black ink on the annual statement but knows that an occasional red-ink season is the test of management stamina.

14.   He takes plenty of advice from the treasurer on investing profits already assured, but as little as possible on the risks of capital expansion for future reward.

15.   He may be a specialist by training, but he is a generalist in spirit and a humanist in his attitude towards life's problems and compensations.

16.   He listens attentively to the playback of grapevine news, but knows that most of it comes from palace-guard chatter.

17.   He tests management potential at all levels with authority as well as responsibility and is always prepared for surprises—some of them favourable.

18.   He believes in law and order, but refuses to be thwarted by tradition—especially when competition gets ahead without it.

19. He admires democracy in principle, but often ignores it in practice, realizing he is a majority of one when the chips are down.

20. Without being a paternalist, he considers his employees, customers, and shareholders as personal charges—and in that order.

21. He is loyal to his community and has a deep sense of social obligation, but refuses to be the whipping boy for the mistakes of civic management.

22. He has strength of character that eschews pomp, bluster, and strut, but he is resolute under any test of ethics or honour.

The Generalist In Top Management

The best captain of a golf club is usually a businessman whose handicap is eighteen when he gets time to play. The best chairman of an airline does much of his piloting on terra firma. He is concerned with the problems of bringing £s into the hangar from passenger and freight traffic in the clouds. A successful top-management man can rise from the ranks of the engineer, the lawyer and the salesman, but when he moves into the top spot he has to check his speciality at the lower level, where it is never forgotten but never obscures the broad administrative panorama that is his essential responsibility.

Modern business has need for the virtues of the cost accountant and methods men in cutting corners, trimming fat from routines and maintaining the tough physique necessary for the competitive fight of the market place. But management never gets to top billing in an industry by saving pennies when the £s are awaiting an invitation to move into the profit column.

There are several broad areas of top-management significance in which profits, growth, prestige and survival are at stake. The sensitivity of modern communication demands an alert eye and decisive hand at the helm. The scope of vision must be worldwide as it weighs incentives and deterrents to overseas investments and commitments. Management needs much of the bargaining skill and a little of the finesse of the diplomat in dealing with people of different languages, customs and trading habits.

Selecting men of management potential is a primary assignment for the leader of a business and with it goes the realization that responsibility should carry a well-defined area of authority. The top manager should be concerned about the trivia that builds upon his desk. Scope in management includes recognition of detail, and the skill to let it find its administrative level.

Managerial Window Dressing

Much has been said about union featherbedding. But what about the sinecures of management? Some executives " in charge of " research, engineering, or public relations—big-name boys with a scientific, educational or military background—are recruited as company window dressing. They may be reputable and competent executives to be sure, but are they justifiable as an expense?

Some foreign businessmen, academic pundits and union leaders think not. They criticize these " flower pots on the window sill " as a wasteful luxury, the useless by-product of a plush era in our economic history. Occasionally, a foreign manufacturer who wears several functional hats will comment on the growing array of executive talent he encounters in English companies. Are these executives, he may ask with good logic, more decorative than useful when salaries are balanced against their contribution to company health and earnings? Are they adding momentum to growth or merely creating an unhealthy bulge in the management veranda?

As the sphere of middle management work is invaded by technology, the performance of managers at this level is measured carefully in terms of service rendered. The cost accountants keep a sharp eye on production and sales, and executives in these divisions must produce or step aside.

For executives in the speculative areas of research and development, standards are more lenient—and with good reason. But when profits permit it, there is the temptation to add a few high-stepping circus horses to the parade. Whether they pull their weight is a matter of conjecture for the stockholders and a matter of conscience for the board of directors.

Management is an individual responsibility, and no top executive can sidestep the finger of blame when an error in judgement has been made. Hiring decisions are no different from product or policy decisions. It is a wise leader who eschews a stable of " company men ". He is wiser still if he knows the stamina of all of his executives under competitive and psychological stress and thinks twice before acquiring names as image makers.

Technology, which is creating turmoil among the crafts, is making equally severe demands on management men. Traditions have been brushed aside by the compelling force of change. In these circumstances it is only fair to expect each executive to pull more than his customary weight. At the same time, he must know the size and importance of the burden. He should be shown at least the perimeters of his task, the goals to be achieved and the ground rules of company policy.

From that point on, his creativity and productivity should be measured in tangible progress. All life is competitive, and there is no excuse for flower pots in the company window when our economy is on trial at home and abroad.

The Coronary Trail

" More people rust out than wear out " is an axiom based on selective judgement. However, there is always the phlegmatic individual whose love of routine immunizes him to the nervous strain that leads to physical disorder. One of the tests of fine administration is good health among key men in company management. The basis of good health—in the years of maturity—is the sensible expenditure of emotional and physical energy.

A good miler paces himself against the timing of the quarter miles to set up reserve strength for the drive towards the tapes. Pacing is equally important in business. The wise manager delegates authority, places confidence in people assigned to key roles, and does not play all the positions on the team. Sophisticated executives take time to rest and to exercise in accordance with the dictates of age and common sense.

The human machine is indeed a thing of wonder, considering the punishment it takes. It gets along with too little or too much, and when it complains, it is often only a mild warning after years of neglect.

The business executive takes greater risks to health of mind and body than does the clerk or craftsman, but he gains little if the risk far exceeds the reward. Pacing oneself is so necessary to the vigorous executive.

Provokers Of Progress

Every age has a curious breed of heroes and martyrs, few of whom wear medals or halos. Necessity and nature seem to create this special kind of men and women as a defence against mediocrity. Not all of them are wise or even logical in their thinking, but they fight for principles and search out the truth as they understand it. They aren't afraid to stick their necks out in public.

These men seldom make history, but they disturb fixed patterns and stimulate social and economic progress. They are the goads and scolds of humanity when it is tempted by the comforts of decay. There are always one or two of them in trade associations, political clubs and university faculties. They are the gadflies, the foes of the *status quo*, the minority voice raised against majority convenience.

Not all of them are good neighbours. Some are busy-bodies who ask embarrassing questions. They are called trouble makers, and with good reason, for they stir up trouble in periods of community neglect. Seen from our own perspectives, they are radical or reactionary, but they are never anchored at dead centre. Not all of them survive success. Some lose their social sting as society accepts their ideas; others may abandon the fight under

23

the pressures of public office or out of pragmatism in a period of changing values which thrusts leadership upon them.

One thing, in any case, is certain: No significant improvement has ever been made in the affairs of mankind without the minority voice of the individual speaking out against group silence or indifference.

Respect for authority is necessary for the proper management of human affairs. But blind conformity to organizational routines, whether in an army or a business, is a dangerous form of loyalty. Man's progress as a gregarious animal owes much of its impetus to the perpetual conflict between the desire for security and the drive for liberty. It is the role of the maverick in society—which includes politics and business—to keep these forces vigorously alive and their conflict forever in ferment.

The heroes and martyrs of this atomic epoch are the men who, refusing to be numbered and bundled together, demand to be named for their ideas, opinions and principles. Some of them are in the union ranks. These men risk their necks when they insist on increased productivity for increased wages and fringe benefits, and when they speak out against wild-cat strikes. Others in top management practise what they preach about competition. Still others, in government, serve with a sense of dedication and without public applause.

No age lacks these needlers of the crusty conscience. They serve as irritants of the lazy mind and burrs in the hair of the appeasers, the conformists, and the neutralists. Around them nothing is normal or routine, and the world is better off for their presence—that is, as long as they stay in the minority.

Management In The High Street

The " average businessman " doesn't exist for long in the competitive climate of the market place. The annual withdrawals from business, whether by choice or by bailiffs notice, are an expensive phase of commercial life. There are too many commercial enterprises on record, and there always will be as long as any man is free to risk his capital, his skills and his stamina as a processor or distributor of goods or as a purveyor of services. Can the marginal operator be salvaged out of the discard? Yes —in many instances by personal discipline and training.

In what way is an entrepreneur, whether a proprietor of a shop or a small factory, any different from a professional (doctor, lawyer, engineer) or a craftsman (machinist, electrician, carpenter)? The difference is not physical, but emotional. The businessman is the most independent, if not always the wisest, man in the High Street. Unlike the professional man, he has no diploma of excellence or certificate of qualification in his chosen work. Unlike the craftsman, he has no union to fight his cause or insure his income against competition.

The basic weakness among the risk-takers in the High Street is lack of management skill in their chosen trade, a fact that accounts for the high casualty rate among small businessmen. One indicator of the financial

25

troubles of these risk-takers is constant activity of the sign painters and installers of neon display lights.

There are three indispensable virtues necessary for the independent merchant: a basic knowledge of the line in which he is engaged, a fundamental understanding of sales psychology in serving old customers and attracting new ones, and a thorough appreciation of the economics of money-handling, from pricing of merchandise to the accumulation of capital reserve. He also must know the delicate point of balance between an inventory that builds volume and excessive stocks that depreciate on the shelves. There is an old saying that " more businesses choke to death than starve to death." This is countered by the equally important adage, " You can't do business from an empty van."

The point of sale is the critical area for any manufacturer. When the customer smiles or frowns at the invitation to buy, the ink turns red or black depending upon the ability of the retailer to convert stock into a cash or credit sale. It costs more to sell goods than to make them because of the uncertainties at the point of sale, and the cost varies with the talents of the man who purveys the goods. The merchant is often more stubborn about correcting his faults as a marketer than as a manager. He may listen to his accountant on cost-cutting, but retain a secret vanity about his ability to outwit the whims of the customer.

Many men are in business because either through personal obstinacy or a courageous independence, they cannot work for anyone else. The difference between these two qualities is the capacity to back up decisions with logic and an understanding of the basic functions of management. This spells the difference between the " average businessman " and the business man who survives.

26

Overlooking The Obvious

Houdini was an ingenious entertainer, who took great risks in practising his art of trickery. Behind his skill as an illusionist was a profoundly scientific mind and a keen grasp of the application of modern mechanics to intricate physical problems. Houdini matched wits with locksmiths and prison governors, and never failed to escape within the time limit. But he almost failed on one occasion by overlooking the obvious.

The governor who nearly outwitted Houdini used a simple artifice. He placed Houdini in an " escapeproof " cell and closed the door. Houdini tried all his ingenuity on the lock but could get no action from the mechanism. A few minutes before the deadline, in desperation, he tried the knob of the ponderous door. Presto! It opened. It hadn't been locked in the first place.

Sometimes we create our own illusion. Our own most trying problems arc often the results of self-deception. Too many executives are prone to assume the doors are locked against them when the difficulty is actually a mental block.

The four-minute mile was a mental block for generations of athletes, but once the barrier was broken by Bannister, dozens of runners disproved the myth that a four-minute mile is impossible for a human operating under his own power.

The obvious is often overlooked in selling a difficult customer, because the difficulty is an assumption, not a reality. Many a sale has been lost because of an obstacle that never existed. A customer can say " no " a hundred times, but he need say " yes " only once.

There is no one right time to ask for an order, but we overlook the obvious when we pass up any opportunity to get the ink on the contract. Henry Ford was asked by an insurance agent whom he had known for many years why he never got any of Ford's business, and Ford merely stated the obvious: " You never asked me."

When envy builds a chill wall between two men in management competition, the obvious reason is often ignored. Instead, a false issue—usually some petty personal issue—is enlarged in self-justification. Most of the time, getting along with people is the art of doing the " obvious thing ", of being considerate, accessible and friendly when we could be cynical or arrogant. But the obvious is overlooked by people who always assume there is another way.

Books And The Business Man

It's a poor manager of his leisure who allows no time for adventure in books. We usually find time for the things we want to do, no matter how demanding the day's work or the evening's social schedule. A book is a patient object, always willing to wait and to serve. No man is rich, no matter how successful, unless his assets include the possession and active use of the wealth that books provide.

Mere literacy is no guarantee of wisdom, no more than a crowded bookshelf is proof of cultural enterprise. The mind of the typical business man soaks up thousands of words daily from newspapers, business papers, and magazines—worthy and necessary servants of his material welfare. Yet, there comes a time, too, for mental recreation and intellectual searching beyond the problems of the moment. What shall a man read in the narrow portion that belongs to his spirit? The choice is his.

A volume of history or biography widens horizons by destroying the urgency of such words as *now*, *today*, and *this year*. Such reading makes us part of centuries and millennia—we study the actions of mankind in a mirror reflecting our ambitions, hopes and faults.

Some executives back away from the word philosophy,

but this tool of the mind is a constant, if unrecognized, companion. The business mind that lays plans for building factories, buying and distributing goods, and performing services uses the creative talents of philosopher, poet and novelist. The more an executive reads for aesthetic pleasure, the more he benefits from the new light that is cast on old problems, and the greater insight he acquires into values which cannot be measured except by the intangibles of the spirit.

An executive cannot afford to bypass libraries and bookstalls with the excuse, " I'm too busy." However cramped for time he is, there's always time left over—for contemplation and for appraisal of one's progress as manager of one's cultural welfare.

It took centuries of blood and ink to produce a free press. Why not value and enjoy the benefits it has brought us? People who burn books are less dangerous to our cultural freedom than people who ignore them.

PART II

Excellence

Art, Craft, And Conscience

Over the centuries, pride in skill has been the badge that identifies true craftsmen. Builders of bridges, castles, and cathedrals have converted the sketches of architects from two dimensions to three. Muscled smiths have tempered steel to the strength of the famed Toledo blades. The old cabinet makers shaped wood to works of compelling grace in home and church. Printers made the alphabet a thing of beauty. Potters, weavers, and engravers plying their trades, chose apprentices of integrity as well as talent.

Men who belonged to the medieval guilds looked upon each assignment as an opportunity to excel. The treasures of metal, wood, stone, and glass are testimony of loyalty to high standards. If the hand skills of artisans have lost some of their character and lustre in our day, the industrial revolution of the 19th century is partly to blame. Yet, regardless of production schedules or union restrictions, carpenter, machinist, die maker, stone mason, and engraver still have the opportunity to add to craftsmanship. In factories where inflation and indifference have lowered the standards of many crafts, the individual can fight against the levelling influence of average performance.

We should not abuse the machine, which has multiplied the comforts and luxuries of life and placed them within the reach of so many, but there is still room for more conscientious effort at lathe, press, loom, and every other aid to mass production. The relative talent of the bulldozer operator will appear in the grading of a slope. His touch at the controls should be as sensitive in its way as that of the jeweller installing a hair spring, or the seamstress threading a needle.

There is no product shaped by any sequence of power tools that pride of craftsmanship cannot improve. Even automation requires high levels of skill and judgement. Quality control is essential. Despite temptations to meet competition or beat inflation by skimping on details, there *is* a market for quality.

It is well to recall that "manufacture" in its Latin origin means "hand-made." That the machine has opened doors to a vast consumer's market is no justification for shoddy performance by production managers and craftsmen. "Quality" is still a term of importance on a warranty, and honesty continues to be an intrinsic quality of the true artificer, whatever his product. For him, "good enough" fails to pass the test of conscience.

Excellence In Government

Never has the need for superior talents in top government positions been more pressing than today. The few appointees who may be seeking political sinecures are quickly disillusioned once they discover the full scope of the job, or they are sidetracked before much time or tax money is squandered on them. Today, we recognize the fact that mediocre performance in governmental positions is not good enough. Inspired judgement and the wisdom of experience are necessities in this world of domestic and international tensions. Although the results may be judged by different sets of balance sheets, the same basic principles of management apply to planning and performance in public administration as in business.

As John Gardner observes in *Excellence: Can We Be Equal and Excellent Too?*: " The society which scorns excellence in plumbing because plumbing is a humble activity and tolerates shoddiness in philosophy because it is an exalted activity will have neither good plumbing nor good philosophy. Neither its pipes nor its theories will hold water."

In terms of the number of people employed and total purchases, the Government is the country's biggest business. Its " profits " are reflected in those services and
34

facilities which contribute to the welfare of the nation's " stockholders "—its people.

A high sense of responsibility at the executive level of government tends to become a model of behaviour for tens of thousands of persons working in the descending scale of the vast mechanism of service to the taxpayer and citizen.

Mere tenure does not shield the laggard or shirker and plenty of them exist in the official family as well as in the routines of industry and trade. However, the negative aspect attracts more attention than the positive and the black sheep is always more visible than the white. The devotion of many a competent public servant to his work is often obscured by the sheer weight of size and numbers. These loyal people in government activities are not asking for the limelight on an appointed task when duty dictates what must be done in the name of public service, and the common good.

Black Figures And Red Faces

"We're in the black." What does this mean? Is it evidence of management skill and sales ingenuity, or is it a deceptive cover-up for inept direction of a business? Many a venture fighting an unfavourable trend, a change in style, customer whims, or new raw material resources can show a loss without apology; its cause and effect are apparent, and a change of pace or direction is in order. But black ink can be a pleasant delusion.

Flood tide covers many a marine hazard, and the real test of navigation comes with the ebb in shoal water. Charting a business course calls for all the mixed prudence and risk of a helmsman. Red ink on the statement is informative, if not consoling. It demands correction and perhaps a change of targets. But black ink can be a curtain for error unless the curtain becomes translucent under the glare of comparative data. This spotlight is especially effective when turned on sales territories in which the market potential is vague and sales staff may not be getting a fair share of the available orders. Sometimes, the cream-skimming star salesman is actually the low producer. Only adequate knowledge of the market for a particular product can determine the relative merits of the salesman, measured against other salesmen of his own company and against competitors.

36

A tough competitive year has its disciplinary benefits for any organization. It's like a shakedown cruise against complacency; structural fitness and operating efficiency are tested in rough weather. The greater the stress, the more apparent is the relative strength or weakness of men and machinery. Neither government nor business welcomes a minor recession but the unexpected squall on the business horizon puts the helmsman on notice.

Red ink is the enemy of routine that clutters up progress. It leaves an embarrassing stain on the hand at the controls and frequently identifies the man accountable for decisions or lack of them. In the accelerated pace of business—with better research in materials and market acceptance, with clarified and pinpointed centres of distribution, with automated facilities for production, with computer controls for stock movement—the margin for personal error narrows perceptibly for any manager with a profit responsibility. With each sector of management in sharp focus, there is less patience or probation for weak management.

As technology and psychology move closer together in business management, the foggy areas of finance, research, processing and marketing are disappearing, and the blind spots for decision-making grow smaller. If " red ink " demands a reason from the accountable manager, " black ink " also requires more specific explanation of the degree of gain, and not necessarily measured against a previous year. If circumstances alter cases as well as profit-and-loss figures, then praise or blame should be calculated against specifics instead of totals. Too much valuable guidance data filters through the porous financial statement, information that should be applicable to a current decision. It's one thing to be " in the black "; it's something else to be in the dark on the profit potential of a business.

What's Happening To Standards?

The price of folly is always high, but many are willing to pay it for the moment's gain. Are you?

There are growing numbers of complaints that inspections are being downgraded and personal services eliminated. This is more frequent in a seller's market when goods may be in demand or short supply. Are lowered standards an inevitable by-product of the inflationary pressures of rising material and labour costs?

By rule-of-thumb measurement, one complaint cancels a hundred compliments—and receives more attention than it merits. But when complaints about quality of product and service gain momentum, it is time to take heed. For a discussion of current complaints let us look first at the retailing function, then at the processing of merchandise.

Self-service is a natural offset to the wage spiral. As a time and space-saver, it is a desirable development for such pre-packed items as groceries, toiletries, and gift items. Self-service is not, however, effective in the marketing of major appliances. The success of " do-it-your-self " is no justification for shifting the service responsibility from dealer to consumer. In too many cases, where self-service cannot take the place of the retail sales clerk, salesmanship has degenerated into order-taking by a poorly informed, lackadaisical staff.

Buyers of new cars have complained of improper servicing on delivery. Confronted by a loose bolt, a badly fitting panel, a squeaking door, the dealer blamed the factory and the factory blamed the dealer.

The retailer may get something different in specification or quality from what he ordered. The blame is hard to place. Was it the customer's lack of clarity in ordering, the salesman's carelessness, the stock clerk's laxity, or the company's policy of making unwarranted substitutions? Facts are lost in a welter of alibis, face-saving excuses, and plain fabrications, causing growing dissatisfaction in many markets.

Pressures, whether volcanic or economic, usually erupt at the weakest point. The questions " What can we do without?" and " What will hurt the least?" are asked when costs move inexorably upward. The erosion of standards by a slow rust of " Why bother?" and " Who cares?" threatens the reputation of both products and services. What are we doing about it?

Many companies are striving to maintain quality standards in products and service. Others have to be reminded that guarantees and reputations are obligations and assets not to be ignored out of laziness or under the duress of rising costs. There is urgent need for strengthening quality control, not only of what we do in manufacturing and in other physical operations, but of what we say in advertisements, catalogues, product specifications, and sales presentations.

Difficulties in meeting competition, domestic or foreign, often tempt the processor to cut corners. Competition serves a good purpose when it causes us to eliminate needless details, but it provides no lasting benefit when it reduces quality or utility for the sake of an immediate competitive advantage.

In part, the answer is maintenance of quality control through improved testing, more effective tools, finer inspection and better customer relations. Another need is for leaders of industry and trade to give public testimony of their determination to fortify standards of quality and brush aside excuses for shoddy goods and slovenly services.

Inflation is a sneak thief when it steals values but a saboteur when it undermines standards. Inflation can do lasting damage unless it is arrested in time.

Courtesy

A man went into a shop to make a small purchase. Three assistants were in the store; one was glancing through a catalogue, the second was arranging stock on the shelves, the third was reading a newspaper.

The customer approached the third and stated his request. Without lifting his head from the paper, he pointed across the aisle to the man arranging stock. The customer crossed the aisle, waited for a few moments and repeated his request. He was greeted with " Can't you see I'm busy?" He turned to the assistant turning the pages of the catalogue, and stated his request again. " How many people do you want to serve you?" said the young man, and walked off.

At that moment, a little man came out of the rear, carrying merchandise in cartons. He put them down and asked, " Can I help you?" The customer stated his request for the fourth time and was served with promptness and courtesy. As he paid for his purchase, he told the little man in the dirty overall, " I appreciate your help, and I'd like to tell the proprietor about it." " I am the proprietor," said the man with a wan smile.

Is this case an exaggerated exception, or is it fairly typical of the attitude of many salespeople behind the counter? Generalizations are dangerous, but comparison suggests that sales courtesy varies inversely with the size of the community, and large cities are the worst offenders.

Diplomacy should not be limited to the employees of the Foreign Office. A traveller's lasting impressions of any country come from its people, and especially those who are asked to perform a service. Retail selling is a point of contact that can build goodwill or destroy it.

The life of the retail sales clerk has its irritations, but it can be one of excitement, growth and even profit. Plenty of salespeople display a pleasant, positive point of view towards the customers—who, be it noted, are not always right or pleasant themselves. But far too many sales assistants show an anti-social attitude that just does not belong behind sales counters anywhere.

The Wheelbarrow

Wheelbarrow production is up! There is no better index of the health of industry.

Why? Because it is so close to problems of the individual. The task is pretty evenly balanced between the hub of a single wheel and the energy of two arms.

There are more complicated things in life, for example, thousands of parts to be assembled in a car, aeroplane, or computer. You don't need an instrument board on a wheelbarrow. All you need is a sense of direction.

Steam drives a locomotive, petrol a car, electricity the shaft of the motor, but it only takes a drop of sweat to set a wheelbarrow in motion.

There is something basic about operating a wheelbarrow. It has a direct drive with no loss of power in transmission. Power breakdowns are few, and repairs are a simple matter.

Today, when people are concerned with the complexities of our industrial economy, it is reassuring to consider the wheelbarrow and to know that production is up.

A Matter Of Degrees

Business men are interested in standards. They insist on quality control of materials, performance tests of machinery, and measurement of the craftsman's skills. But when they consider the standards upon which the scientist, the professional man, and the management generalist must be judged, the end often gets confused with the means. This confusion is especially apparent when the educational assets of a candidate for employment or promotion are being considered.

In recent years, personnel directors have tempered their attitude towards the university degree as an over-all measurement of a young man's talents. They look for other indications of character, growth and intellect of the whole man, especially in selecting candidates with managerial potential.

A degree in business administration, science, humanities, medicine, law or divinity is evidence of time, energy, and intelligence applied to self-improvement. It is also a recognition of achievement, as measured by established standards of excellence in the field. As a basis for the recruitment of technicians and social scientists, the university degree is a necessary and highly desirable criterion. Degrees in economics and the humanities are equally

44

significant in the selection of young men with management potential.

In the turbulence of technology, the old school in personnel selection have warped the significance of the university degree by attributing to it a set of values it was never intended to reflect.

Industry needs specialists for technology and research for both our defence needs and in the development of new civilian products. Eventually, some of these men will evolve into candidates for managerial responsibility. But the managers of the future cannot come from these ranks alone. Industry needs just as urgently the well-rounded individual who has the long-term outlook necessary in a good manager. Such a man may have a university degree but—more important than a degree—he has certain human attributes not easily calibrated by letters of the alphabet, identifiable qualities of understanding and compassion that are related to the total human experience.

Effective Management In
A Recession Period

A period of recession brings some blessings if we have the courage and imagination to make the most of the opportunity to appraise our products, equipment, location, and personnel.

There is a right way and a wrong way to go about the job.

In a lean era, we ought to be selective about people, methods, and machines. But if we attack the problem like a lone cane-cutter with a machete, swinging wildly at high-expense items, we are likely to injure morale. The typical employee is sensitive to the consequences of the firm's financial condition. The more he knows about his company's productivity, the quicker he relates it to profits and his pay envelope, and the more readily he will pitch in and help.

When a factory closes down briefly for retooling, it usually chooses a slack season. A lag can offer the manager a chance to measure the output of men and machines. Where efficiency and productivity are high, the fact will stand out in bold relief. Where there is ineptness in supervision and operations, the fault will be equally apparent.

The executive should not waste sentiment on obsolete

facilities. The price of obsolescence is often failure—a higher price than capital investment in new equipment and facilities, even at currently inflated values.

Let's Try A Cruising Speed

Neither man nor machine is designed to operate at peak power indefinitely. Nor is the economy capable of continuous acceleration.

Most men, like most machines, have three basic speeds —maximum, cruising, and idling. We need the reserve power of top speed in an emergency. There are times when it is best to idle without a load to carry or pull. But at the cruising speed we perform best, and we get the best results for our expenditure of fuel.

Maximum demands on men or machines increase the danger from fatigue of mind or metal. The flywheel, the governor, and other stabilizers of energy are designed to give the machine a smooth power flow. In a similar way, the Bank of England regulates the energy of credit to control power pulsation in the national economy.

The test of prosperity is consumption, not production, and the rate of consumption is largely influenced by the public appetite for consumer goods. When the customer grows fearful or abstemious and decides to get along without things, the flow of goods becomes sluggish all along the channels of distribution.

Over-production is often the result of a top-speed policy when a cruising-speed programme would be more profitable. The glutted market destroys current profits and delays future returns. An understanding of consumer psychology is necessary.

To achieve a cruising speed which is less costly and more profitable than alternate peak and idling speeds, we depend on market research—rather than machine capacity—as a guide to sensible manufacturing schedules. We depend on the Bank of England to regulate the flow of credit.

It is important to remember that, in the long run, men and machines give the best account of themselves at cruising speed.

Trade Observations

When seed money is easy to acquire, a lot of wild oats are sown.

When seed money is scarce, land is cultivated behind familiar fences.

When customers are scarce, quality improves, and more services are rendered.

When skills grow scarce and inspection lax, excellence tarnishes with neglect.

When goods are in short supply, the supplier enjoys the luxury of quality risks.

When red ink shows on the annual statement, it is easy to blame the customer, competitor and " conditions."

When the rate of employment sags, productivity is apt to increase, even among executives.

When the flood tide of sales covers up management errors, there's danger ahead.

When prices and wages go up without comparable increase in values, you have inflation.

When goods and services improve with a comparable rise in prices and up-graded productivity, you have an improved standard of living.

When keen competition exists for capital, customers, and jobs, the nation's economy demonstrates a muscular tension that is healthy for all concerned.

PART III

Business Ethics

Business Ethics

Benjamin Franklin is responsible for the wall motto,
" Honesty is the best policy." But was he right? Is honesty a policy or a principle?

Good ethics in the broad sense is amply covered by the
Golden Rule, but broad concepts are not always easy to
apply. In the complexity of world competition, many trying situations arise to test the conscience of the individual. In these situations there can usually be found (1)
an area of debate about the proper ethics, (2) a passive
acceptance of customs or methods which tax ethical definitions, or (3) a flagrant abuse of fact which is inexcus-
able on ethical grounds.

There is scarcely an hour of the day when the business
man is not called upon to make ethical judgements
among employees, customers, shareholders, and the public. Men of strong moral principles make many ethical
decisions instinctively, even when the choice costs them
time, money, or the sacrifice of a temporary advantage
over competitor or neighbour. A really sensitive conscience is even apt to confuse scruples with principles
and give the other fellow the benefit of the doubt.

The dictionary, in defining ethics, as " the science of
moral duty," adds in an explanatory comment: " Abso-

lute ethics affirms an unchanging moral code; relative ethics regards moral rules as varying in the human development." Here is a key to modern problems in ethical behaviour, ethical example, and ethical leadership.

Absolute ethics include the discipline of the spirit. Relative ethics, like regulatory law, is easily amended by circumstance. In business and industrial relations, relative ethical standards advanced a little in the nineteenth century and a lot in the twentieth century. But ethics needs the indignation of the spirit to give added impact to its force on behalf of the rights, privileges and dignity of man.

Behind most ethical offences are the half-truth, the mental reservation, the selective reasoning which weaken the sense of verbal agreement, the understanding of a responsibility. Staying within the law is never a guarantee of acceptable ethical conduct. In fact, the law itself on occasion can and does encourage unethical behaviour. In any vast organization of people, the bewildering impact of numbers makes it difficult to maintain a sharp ethical focus on the rights of the individual. One of the dangers of group decisions is that broad, impersonal judgement lays a heavy hand on the just and unjust, the skilled and unskilled, the energetic and the lackadaisical.

Actually, there is no easy distinction between the morality of the corporation and the morality of the individual. Corporate conscience must be interpreted by individuals.

If an act is legal, is it necessarily ethical? To stay within the law but outside the pale of ethical behaviour is the device of the trickster who uses Blackstone as a shield for his acts of deceit.

Ethical behaviour is concerned with human values, not with legalities. Most law applying to business is regulatory, and often it has nothing to do with civic virtue or commercial rectitude. Gambling is permitted or restricted by the Government. Sunday retail sales are permitted, limited, or forbidden by laws. Here there is no intrinsic problem of good and evil, but rather of public attitude or convenience. Regulatory law is obeyed because it is a legal discipline, not because of inherent principle of virtue. However, no law which is discriminatory, selective in principle, or unjust in design commands respect or even obedience.

The bankruptcy law is a humane instrument by which the penalties of commercial failure are limited. After a bankruptcy composition, some individuals shrug off their obligations and silence conscience with a legal rationalization. Others—and these are in the minority—refuse to hide behind the law. They pay off their obligations even if it takes a lifetime. Here is a clear example of absolute versus relative ethics.

Special tests of ethical fibre in business have multiplied in this period of mergers and acquisitions. Besides the compatible marriage of interests in which the rights of customer, labour, and shareholders are considered, there are also many shotgun marriages in which a competitor is eliminated, a town injured economically, a product shelved, a company raided of its cash, and a loyal staff scattered after years of service. If any individual has a calloused hand, a dull conscience, and an evil eye, it is the merger specialist, who uses a weak, often family-managed company as merger bait for tax-saving purposes or an improvement of his own profits. Anti-monopoly legislation cannot restrain all the shrewd offenders against the moral law.

Some ethical decisions are closely related to basic economic decisions. For instance Company A and Company B produced cars with defective mechanisms. Company A later replaced the faulty parts at a tremendous cost that soaked up much of their annual profits. Company B refused to make good an engineering error, was sued both by customers and dealers and suffered a prolonged business setback.

An electrical appliance company voluntarily wrote to several hundred customers and offered to replace a faulty part without charge. This decision cost a great deal of money but it was worth considerably more in goodwill.

Ethics and guarantees are frequently at odds, especially when a company retreats from claims and complaints behind a thick hedge of small type. On the other hand, there are always dealers and customers who seek a special advantage by returning goods damaged in use rather than in transit.

The moral issue of featherbedding and sweetheart contracts in labour-management relations deserves a chapter to itself, because the moral offence against labour bargaining is a continuous conspiracy in which men play traitors to their fellow-workers. Businessmen who condone the bribe to labour leaders are at a low stage of depravity in industrial relations, lower in fact than the men who take their favours.

Except under the law which guarantees their rights as individuals, people are equal in no respect. One of the ethical difficulties in an industrial democracy is conflict between the urge of superior talent to rise to a higher level and the heavy weight of numbers which tends to pull down that level to mediocrity. In the eyes of any morally sensitive leader, there is a fine distinction between the recognition of talent and the fair treatment of the median of humanity—which is entitled to consideration but not priority.

There is also the perpetual conflict between seniority and ability. Designed as a recognition of loyalty, the seniority rule is often a detriment to progress in manage-

55

ment. Many banks and old-fashioned companies lose able men who refuse to be mere time servers. Any decisions affecting seniority are certain to have significant ethical echoes, with the moral margin favouring the right of a young man to move ahead.

Among the marginal areas of ethics is the relationship of vendor and supplier and the degree of decency with which orders are secured. The Inland Revenue recognises entertainment of actual and prospective foreign customers as a legitimate expense, up to an indefinite point. But where is the point at which the cost of the social softening of a customer by entertainment becomes an ethical offence? Can anyone put a percentage limitation on commercial bribery? Some companies would fire a purchasing agent or an engineer in charge of specifications for pursuing a policy encouraged or winked at by their own sales department.

Although the income tax man recognizes the pragmatism of commercial bribery—whether it be the accepted custom of a dinner, theatre, and night club or the moral turpitude of a direct cash handout—there is good reason to consider the whole range of commercial handouts as unethical. But there is equally good reason to know that it will continue so long as people are more emotional than rational in their judgements.

The income tax law was conceived primarily as a revenue-producing instrument of the Government, with little regard for ethical consequences. It has taught business men many bad habits and led to many marginal decisions. Even the Government can incite dishonesty by the inequities of the law and by favouritism or laxity in its enforcement.

What is ethical conduct, and how do we gauge it? We can consider the answer of Etienne Gilson, the French philospher: " Moral honesty is, at bottom, a scrupulous respect for the rules of justice; intellectual honesty is a scrupulous respect for truth." This standard applies to all men of industry and trade. It calls for rigid honesty in financial negotiations, accurate identification of materials, strict adherence to quality controls in manufacturing, fairness in labour relations, candour in product pricing, honour in warranties, and truth in advertising statements.

The struggle for an ethical standard persists despite all the negative pull for short-term advantage. Ethics in big business, small business, professional life, even the much-criticized area of labour relations has improved under self-criticism and legal restraint. But moral progress is painfully slow, for the primary gain must come through self-discipline rather than legal compulsion. In the areas of good conduct and honest judgement, there is no substitute for personal conscience. When a man is asked to perform a dishonourable act for a superior—whether individual, company, or branch of government—he is bound by conscience to refuse, regardless of the penalty to himself. Many business men have learned that good ethics is also good business. The confidence it creates makes for a sound business relationship.

Personal Accountability

National defence is concerned with a foe, actual, potential or imaginary, beyond our borders. But no amount of physical armament can deal with the danger that lurks within the citizen himself. Is our moral fibre depreciating as the individual becomes less accountable for his conduct? The evidence is disturbing.

What are the complaints to be made in self-appraisal? We can offer several: first, a cynical attitude towards excellence as a badge of character; second, waning discipline towards commitment; third, a shrug of the shoulders towards civic duties.

These complaints are not limited to the warnings of pulpit zealot or professional kill-joy. Let's face the fact that our cobwebbed conscience tends to dim distinctions between expediency and integrity, self-justification and candour.

Management—top, middle or supervisory—is too often willing to accept a " passing average " instead of " excellence " in judgement of its own work and that of its laggard craftsmen. This relates to the practice of planned obsolescence, poor standards of inspection and take-it-or-leave-it salesmanship.

Abuse of privilege is flagrant in official, private and

professional life—as prevalent among educators, lawyers, and doctors as among business and labour leaders. Fortunately, there still is a core of humanity that draws its sap from the roots of sacrifice. It includes the selfless, whose nobility of character needs no fanfare— men and women who are found among the humble as well as the exalted. It is to them that we must look for reassurance in a day of doubt.

Every man is accountable for his acts under the laws of the land, but also *accountable for acts of omission* under the natural law that demands we meet our obligations to our neighbours, the community, the country and the world in which we live. If there is a national deficit in the intangible assets of character, we must learn what is wrong and correct the weakness. This is a pertinent question, and each of us is accountable for an honest answer.

The Liberal Thinker In Business

Can a business man be a liberal thinker?

Why not? The roots of trade are in the liberal tradition. Commerce led Europe out of the feudal shadows of the Middle Ages. The rise of the common man ran parallel to the enterprise of the commercial traveller in Europe. Practically every colony was a business venture underwritten by men with a view to monetary reward for their risk. There certainly were social, political, and religious freedoms involved in these enterprises, but the hopes of their leaders rested heavily on the support of risk capital.

The English business man is liberal when he is willing to recognize potential merit in the foreign trader's ideas, products, and techniques, even though they may be new to him and not always easy to accept. He is liberal when he makes intelligent allowance for the language, customs, and methods of overseas customers or competitors. He is liberal when he considers the impact of his decisions on his employees, customers, shareholders, vendors, and the people in the community in which he has factories and offices.

The liberal thinker does not tend to see people as " good " and " bad ". He knows that some disagreements are the result of honest differences of opinion, and he is willing to consider the evidence, and make his own judgement on the facts presented.

The liberal business man keeps informed of the political, social, and economic progress of his community. He recognizes the need for regulatory laws. He also takes action when his rights and those of his competitors are unfairly restricted. The liberal does not say, " I'm staying out of politics." He knows his responsibility as a citizen and never sidesteps it.

The liberal in business respects the courage of an honest opponent, whether labour leader or competitor. If there are two sides to a question, he tries to find the right side and stay off the fence. He knows that all ideas, things, and people have dimensions and limitations, and there comes a time when principles have to be defined and accepted. He knows that no man is liberal who attempts to be all things to all people—not even in business when profits are at stake.

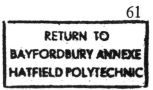

PART IV

Social Responsibility

The Scars Of Progress

Urban slums are the scars of progress. Every city in England has its blight in varying degrees. Most of it is inherited from the industrial expansion of communities in the brash days of mass production, early power tools and haphazard population growth of the late nineteenth century, and from the sustained impulse of war and defence economies of the first half of the twentieth century. The price of present prosperity is a large debt of embarrassment and inflated costs for the future. Part of this debt belongs to opportunists who live for the present and ignore the need for long term planning for industry locations, trade centres, housing, schools and recreational centres. Civic improvements with intelligent planning are investments in time that are often ignored by the " penny wise and pound foolish." The selfish and short-sighted policies of pragmatists in city growth multiply the debt of error to posterity and at a rapidly accelerating rate.

The sins of the fathers are not only measured in slums, lack of transportation facilities and haphazard roads, but also in a tendency to avoid basic remedies with past work-substitutes. Nor can the responsibility for urban renewal be unloaded on the government when the cause and cure may be a local problem. But a repair job is urgent. Our bulging cities with their dead centres are faced with steadily declining rate values among low-income and no-income families and surrounding properties.

There is no justification in blaming middle-class families for escaping to the suburbs and taking some light industry and trade centres with them. To this movement belongs the natural evolution of society, and the complex pressures of technology, professional talents, trade skills, and the physical and cultural reach for "something better." We can't change human nature, but self-help in the cities is the first corrective step in making safe, livable, self-reliant neighbourhoods.

To what extent is industry responsible to the community in which it produces goods and services, and provides jobs? There was a time when industrial adventurers moved into a community, used its physical resources, hired and fired with impunity, played little or no part in civic programmes, and moved out when it suited the convenience of the management, often leaving the raw wounds of its abuse of nature and harsh memories of the people it displaced. But in the middle of the twentieth century, a more sensitive breed of management has recognized that human values comes first and the profit system must include a responsibility to society as well as shareholders.

The new factories visible from our main highways often blend into the surroundings, giving an air of distinction to the site selected by the proprietors. Factory design has kept abreast of the best functional concepts, offering operating efficiency to the owner as well as visual pleasure to employee, townsman and traveller. Nevertheless, many of our cities and small industrial towns are still blotched and maimed by brick rectangles of the 1890s with dingy windows, and surrounding slums. It may take a generation to get rid of these op-

E   65

pressive reminders of a crude era of smoke, noise, dust, and pollution of air and water.

Civilization began at the crossroads when nomads met, pooled their resources, and stopped roaming. That's where cities took root, and order moved in for the common good, and government began to evolve. The city is father to the state, and the state is father to the nation. Reclamation of the decayed hearts of the business and industrial communities is necessary if we are to revitalize the tax structure and wipe out the festering areas of civic shame. But self-help is the generating force of improvement which attracts the eye of the investor, the entrepreneur, the resident and the aesthete.

Men, Morality, And Management

Good leadership is a major activity of the professional manager. When it is applied to a company or any organization, whether military, social, or religious, it calls for more risk than prudence, more understanding than tact and more principle than expediency.

Despite all the democracy associated with the free enterprise system, and the selection, training, and advancement of managers, the company enjoys the continuity of a monarchy and some of its regal aspects of authority.

Moral responsibility begins at the top and filters down through middle management and supervisors. It includes the complex and relative ethics of wages, work rules, seniority, fringe benefits, profit participation, and pensions. It includes a proper estimate of the worth of technology, research and specialists in staff assignments.

Morality is the same, whether management faces the consuming public, the shareholder, or the staff. It begins with self respect.

What then are the dimensions of the moral framework in which the manager functions?

The manager begins by recognizing the need for order. Man's identification of self as the centre of movement in an orderly universe begins with his recognition of the job at hand and the need to meet his obligations.

The morality of management can be summed up in a single ethical responsibility and conveyed in seven basic " senses " which begin with man, the individual, not mankind as a generalization. Man, the individual, must have:

1. A sense of identity.
2. A sense of order.
3. A sense of purpose.
4. A sense of power.
5. A sense of love.
6. A sense of dignity.
7. A sense of time.

Many leaders are concerned with the *sense of identity*, for modernity tends to dim the identity of the individual, his meaning as a person, his duty as a citizen, his significance as a thinking being.

The difficulty with life in an industrial democracy, with its political complexities and its social confusions, is that it tends to reduce the individual to a number and to define human behaviour in terms of averages. Joseph Stalin is credited with having said, " The death of one man is a tragedy, the death of a million is a statistic." In a democracy, the tendency is to level people to a statistical oblivion; yet humanity rebels against averages.

The human equation does not respond to the rigidity of mathematical equations. The man in management identifies the individual, who, in our world of mass movements, tidal surges of population, and electronic memory, faces a continuing struggle between name and number.

Management also seeks the numerical discipline which implies a *sense of order*—the statistic, the index number, wage rates, operating ratios, Gross National Product, and other measuring devices for production, sales, and profits. Yet excessive use of this discipline sets up a complexity which can invite chaos. Regulatory law seeking to ensure justice and fair play often creates as many new legal and social snarls as it untangles. Justice is sometimes trapped in a maze of its own design.

Most regulatory law is a matter of group discipline rather than moral restraint. It is part of the price society pays for being civilized. The company manager is faced with many restrictions and limitations under national laws and local ordinances, He cannot follow the dictates of conscience alone. Yet the manager patiently submits to the legal chafing for the common good—and accepts the need for order in social behaviour—though there are times when *he feels like Gulliver in Lilliput, tied down by a web of minor restraints* which are a major handicap to the free movement of business.

The sense of purpose in man's earthly adventure is often overlooked in the pragmatism of daily need. Again, the individual dims into the group, and his significance as a name, a face, a soul is lost in the temporary demands of the job. Humanism suggests that the world's work be done, but not at the expense of a man's loyalty to his code of personal ethics or his freedom of decision within legal bounds.

The sense of purpose includes aesthetics for those who have the capacity to enjoy the arts as participants, critics, or spectators. It also includes the right to ignore the arts and proclaim the negative right to any form of indolence or unproductive recreation which pleases a man's fancy. The purposes of life, in the main, are worthy and serious, and it is a manager's responsibility to point to the signs on the doors. It is up to the individual to select the knobs.

Man's *sense of power*, growing in magnitude, is offset by his anxiety about whether it will be applied for improvement or immolation. Man has seen power in the past fifty years exceed all the dynamics of transport and communication of the past 5,000 years. His voice circles the earth in an instant. He has touched sea bottom,

69

leaped into space, walked on the moon, and exceeded most living things in nature at their own arts and in their own environment, whether on land, in the sky, or under water. Yet man recognizes that the power of the printed and spoken word exceeds the power of the atom in influencing minds and hearts.

The power of modern capitalism over the lives of people grows with the complexity of our industrial civilization. Use and abuse of this power rest equally with industrial management and labour leaders, both of whom often ignore the rights of the majority in the tensions of industrial strife. The power of the agencies of communication—newspapers, magazines, radio and TV—strains at the moral margins in attempting to influence opinion and conscience.

Company power has invited the discipline of anti-monopoly laws. Labour power has brought increasing legal controls. It was Lord Acton who said, " Power tends to corrupt; absolute power tends to corrupt absolutely." Man, in re-examining his power potentials, has reason to be fearful of his gifts.

The *sense of love* is still the basic hope of justification for the human race.

Yet the spirit of " my brother's keeper " holds within it the danger that " my brother " will seek security at the expense of his sense of risk and competitive spirit. When a man's food, shelter, and education are all provided for, there is a weakening of the spine and a numbing of the will. The meaning of " my brother's keeper " is not the possessive one of a friendly but insistent jailer.

Despite all the wars of nations, the degradation of captives, and the enslavement of millions of serfs, the *sense of dignity* in man persists because of the recurring spirit of rebellion against slavery of mind or body. Even when the ankles of men are fettered, their minds fight free of the brainwash and unmask the sophistries of their tormentors.

The drudgery is fast disappearing from farm and factory. But with the machine, mass-production, and automation, the dignity of labour faces a challenge, for man could easily be enslaved by the slave he created to serve him.

The pulse is a constant reminder of the *sense of time*, which encourages, as well as limits, the scope of man's achievement. *Everything must be done under the compulsion of time*, and yet it is obvious that most people are but shadows on the sundial. The achievements are by the few, the honours for the few. Yet the busy man finds time, time to ask questions that have no simple answers.

There is one school of managers, and not necessarily the old school, which believes its responsibility should begin and end with the company balance sheet. Another school of wider scope and higher sights sees the company score card, including the status of the company, measured in public opinion as a positive or negative influence in the community. A third group, growing more vocal, if not altogether lucid in statement, is groping for a concept of deeper spiritual dimension. This group is increasingly sensitive to the manager's duty in defending the moral stamina of a people whose behaviour is mirrored before a world audience. These managers find it difficult to accept the distorted image created by business and political leaders who ask others at home and abroad to " Do as I say, not as I do."

Our managers must accept greater moral responsibility of leadership as the earth shrinks, and elbows bruise in the scramble for advantage in world markets. The image of the English trader in other lands is the composite of management overseas. It is up to industrial leaders to pick men who are acceptable in any market place or at any crossroads of diplomacy.

These men are aware of something imminent—indefinable in words, intangible in shape—the presence of which becomes even more apparent as technology increases. The " something " is not the terror of the atom in fission or fusion, nor any dire potential of the chemistry of nature. Rather, it is the awesome premise that we can go on indefinitely creating, processing, converting, consuming to the formula of material growth without a corresponding enlargement of the spirit and an increased enlightenment of the human intellect.

The manager of vision has the extrasensory perception to feel and fear the world of the great god Gadget. Science and the marvels of the natural world are his servants, not his masters—or his toys.

As a humanistic leader, he is primarily concerned with the welfare of man. He is fearful of the " isms " that endanger the future; cynicism, opportunism, and hedonism. These are imminent threats to man's moral stamina.

Modern management is confronted by high-propped illusions of grandeur, a world on stilts that is weakened by defeatist attitudes towards truth and virtue—the shrug of shoulders by many citizens in high places; public officials, captains of industry, union leaders, men who debase the Golden Rule with their lack of integrity. The perceptive manager, however, recognizes the crying need for candour.

Fortunately, company leaders of high repute in public and private life are still in control of the business conscience. The margin may be slim at times but they are confident that good ethics will prevail, despite the protective callous on the hides of many men. A leader with integrity cannot adjust his ethics to the season, the situation, or the person, but must, instead, be guided by principle—even when its hurts his pride or purse.

72

Academics And
The Counting House

The relationship of education and business is both tandem and tangent as a sophisticated society drives them closer together in a marriage of convenience that has some elements of romance. Higher education today is concerned not only with agricultural and industrial problems, but with urban ones as well. The educator, asking for a more dynamic role in the hurly-burly, is moving further away from the insular tradition of a university shelter. Neither educator nor businessman can be self-sufficient in his new state of constant association. Yet, the educator may have to fight for recognition as an equal under the so-called free enterprise system.

One may ask, what are the objectives of education in a heterogeneous, open society? Who pays the educator and is the compensation adequate? Who manages higher education and how does the organization structure of the university differ from that of industry? How does authority in education differ from the chain of command in factory and counting house? How are our pragmatic, aesthetic, and ethical values balanced?

It is apparent that modern education, through applied research, has attempted to meet the demands of government and industry. It has accelerated the conquest of

73

nature with new fuels for power, faster wheels, keels, wings and instruments of communication, more effective manufacturing and marketing techniques and an endless variety of services. Automation, computerization and the refinements of mechanization have become an integral, professional concern of the professor.

A decade ago, Cassandras were crying that Russian science had gone ahead of the world with determined strides. The cry for science at the expense of arts programmes was heard everywhere. The sophistry in that cry is now apparent as Russia becomes critical of its intensive scientific blitz, and corrective curricular revisions are being made in the U.S.S.R. The Russian poets and philosophers have gained enough courage to criticize purely mechanistic ideals and pantries of tasteless ideological sawdust. Human values are now reasserting themselves in the spirit of such Slavic humanists as Gorky.

Education should be an adventure in metaphysics before it becames indentured to the laws of physics. Education must build on philosophic premises related to Twentieth Century survival before it adds to the solitude of the ivory or iron towers. It should search for sustenance not only in college halls but in the grass roots regions where the dynamics of wisdom are generated. Although it maintains basic principles, education must also adapt its performance to the pressure of change.

Business, too, is changing. Today it has a more responsible attitude towards society than it had when the Victorian age used a big stick and labour was only grudgingly accepted as a human asset and not a mere commodity. Still, university dons tend to distrust businessmen.

Emissaries of industry seeking interviews with graduates who have management potential report a persistent chill in the liberal arts climate. Young men, who may have their education financed in part by taxes imposed upon business, are encouraged to seek the status of the professions rather than the market place.

University heads must be familiar with community and government relations and with finance. Often they have to discuss with industry the details of mutual responsibility in setting up systematic fiscal programmes for revenues and expenditures. Today, there is just as much management talent required in big education as in big business. This need expands in proportion to the ever-escalating number of students and the equally expanding cost of facilities, and teaching staff.

Management in industry has matured enough to ask management in education, questions about school objectives, policies and facilities. Business management seeks information about the financing of education, teachers freedom of expression, student attitudes and behaviour. Education, for its part, has a right to know why these questions are being asked.

Fortunately, the " mix " of educator and industrial executive has begun to dissipate the fog emanating from inherited antagonisms. " On the job " crossbreeding of education and industry in co-operative research projects imbues mutual enthusiasms and respect.

Relationships between all levels continue to require study. Current management distinctions often shunt a man to a plateau from which there is little chance of escape. Many a chemist, engineer or accountant has spent years on the side-track. It is here that the accent on liberal arts and the behavioural sciences comes to the aid of the specialist who has ambitions to enter higher levels of management. These disciplines strengthen the candidate's resources in dealing with human relationships.

Tensions between educator and businessman may be

little more than family feuds. These diminish as mutual problems of survival appear, accelerating the "danse macabre" of contemporary civilization. Bickering serves to clear the air, and understanding may come with revised opinions. The first step requires that both parties exhibit the will to be understood in a dialogue with *ad hoc* definitions. It is high time for educator and businessman to speak the same language. There is no problem that cannot be clarified in basic English.

Neutralism In Business

Today we have in the world three political groups, the Communist Eastern bloc, the capitalist Western bloc, and the neutralists who sit on the side lines wavering in support of either side as they watch the struggle for economic and political superiority.

Neutralism is not limited to diplomacy, where it may have the excuse of self-preservation. It can be observed in business management that avoids decisions when principle or risk of money, energy, or time is involved. "*Status quo*—do not disturb" is the policy of these companies. They fail to take a stand on legislative issues, regulatory disputes, or community problems. They are not engaged and, therefore, not exposed to the challenge of criticism on matters of principle.

Neutralism in business is typified by the wait-and-see policy which plays it safe—and occasionally winds up out of the game. In a recession, neutralism waits for a trend to follow instead of creating a trend by providing leadership. It depresses confidence and increases the negative sentiment which atrophies the mind and muscle of business. It seldom makes errors—except the big error of omission. More companies falter and fall by the wayside because of paralysed imagination than because they

77

took a calculated risk.

Life demands more daring than caution. When an individual, company, or nation places total security above reasonable risk, it accepts a vegetable existence and sacrifices integrity and purpose to conformity. " Dare a little and doubt a little, but have a lot of faith " is good counsel when we are called on to make a decision. Every change in the economy offers opportunities to alert an enlightened management.

Internationally, we have been pushed off balance by political antagonists and aggressive competitors. But we can't complain of the increasing neutralism at the United Nations when we, as business men, permit this disease to infect our attitudes in dealing with our own problems. There comes a time when we can't " abstain " from voting for or against, when we can't be silent to escape being counted when a principle is at stake.

Too often, neutralism is a technique for side-stepping responsibilities and dismissing obligations. No man can face life's challenges by saying " I'm not here." British business grew powerful by assuming risks and facing issues decisively. Its progress will stop if management refuses to take an active interest in policies, attitudes, or legislation affecting the welfare of industry at home and abroad. There is little room for neutrals in business. Neutralism creates nothing. It is sterile.

The Ultimate

The dead soldier is replaced by a generation of forgetting after each war. Recrimination is brief, promises fade, and treaties are broken as new circumstances create new allies and new enemies. Ideals grow dim in the dust of the mottoes rubbed from the facade of public buildings. Although men are mortal, man lives on in endless links. Life gestates from seed to fruit in nine months. The fighting man matures in eighteen years; the thinking man—well, that requires reflection.

Men are replaced more quickly than the material they consume in their quarrels and destroy in their vengeance. The creation of matter is measured in the light years of a star cooling in the deep shadows of the night. The making of coal, oil and other fuels is measured in the countless millennia of decay and change.

Man, a recent invader of earth's surface, is a vessel of clay shaped and reshaped to a creature of wonder, splendour and terror. He tortures nature for her secrets, acquires powers beyond his understanding and control and seeks to direct, ennoble and discipline these forces to his will.

In ten thousand years of recorded history, man's path is marked by confusion, frustration, insensate curiosity and unmistakable progress. He alternately submits to conscience and recants. He suspects a divine impetus to the adventures of his mischievous mind which strains at authority, snarls at tradition, and gnaws at the leash which binds the flesh and the spirit.

Life, the mysterious phenomena of the natural order, tells many secrets to the inquiring eye, but not the secret of man's purpose. Man still hasn't learned the meaning of his savage lust for power in a world of microcosm and macrocosm. Eternity and infinity are endless strings of speculation—daily need measured in units of time and space.

As man approaches the apex of material triumphs of the scientific mind, he is becoming increasingly aware of the necessity for a stock figure and evaluation of his social, political and spiritual gains.

Man is faced with many questions, and each solution opens upon new corridors of locked doors and blank panels. If the challenge taunts and curiosity rankles, he hopes for a moment of meditation and recapitulation to assess his achievements. Sometimes, with his questioning, come answers to questions he has not asked.

If " the proper study of mankind is man," then man comes first—his survival, his welfare, and his sense of purpose. The last is the most significant and often the least considered, for the tyranny of time has caused the things that matter to matter least.

Man has begun to realize that the mere satisfaction of the need for creature comfort and personal and group security leads only to mediocrity and the mass anonymity of numbers. Slowly he concedes that the vitality of the individual springs from his ideas and his ideals.

Man has learned with some reticence that existence is competitive and that, when people are treated as equals, they don't respond equally to such treatment. Out of the variants of human qualities he holds the rising of leaders —philosophers, teachers, prophets, idealists including the martyrs for just causes and the demagogues in search of power.

There have always been crises in the affairs of men in their long climb out of the depths of slavery and savagery. Men have suffered and died for just and unjust causes, and out of their loins new men have risen, good and bad. Each crisis has differed somewhat in nature and intensity as science has provided more light for the journey. If progress is represented as a triangle, man is moving towards its apex with accelerating speed. There is the frightening awareness of an approaching climax in our political, economic and social destinies. We are increasingly aware of a terminal point. All of this is associated with the splitting of the atom, the conquest of gravity and the puncturing of the space ceiling.

Where do we go from here? What can we do as legislators, merchants, scientists or teachers to meet the emergency?

There is a cynical proverb that the evil in man is always equal to the opportunity to use it, and time will provide the incident for its most sinister application. There is also the inner voice which promises that man's capacity for good outweighs his evil impulse, and will conquer the dark genie who has his hand on the switch to perdition.

The clawing at the veil of life goes on with frantic speed under the compulsion of time, with men seeking for meaning and understanding. We use nature's laws and forces to pry open her cache of mysteries and employ them against her. But the key to man's purpose in the cosmic scheme is still not visible.

The secret lies between the womb and the tomb, and life goes on. The dead soldier is resurrected in eighteen

F

years, and the dying concepts of liberty, justice, and peace are revived with them. So too, the aspirations for power as definitions of liberty, justice, and peace are warped into masks for leaders who seize these symbols to disguise their selfish intentions.

But although man is mortal, he shares divinity in segments of time and as long as the cry of birth is heard, the song of hope persists for his ultimate redemption as a creature of flesh and spirit.

Back To The Caves

Primitive man was a cave dweller. Fear, food and family were his interests as he clawed his way through ignorance towards understanding. Sophisticated man may also be a cave dweller. Fear, food and family are again his interests as he stumbles into the blinding sun of a science devoid of self-discipline.

So the first man and the last may be troglodytes, holed up in the shadows of a mind that could conquer space but not its own search for power.

Some men go blind peering into darkness, some from staring into light.

PART V
Business Concepts

Credit

Credit is a form of money, minted of faith. It is as old as man's willingness to honour the word of his fellow man. Credit is not a right, but a privilege earned by candour and restraint. It flourishes with prudent use; it fades with neglect and abuse.

We live in a credit motivated economy, and we find credit one of the more worthy symbols of our industrial civilization. Credit moves quietly and constantly beneath the daily routines of family, business community and international trade. Credit is an expression of man's faith in the future, his ability to perform a service within the specified period of time.

Where there is credit, there is the hazard of loss as well as the opportunity for gain. The candour of the applicant is as necessary to the decision as the willingness of the grantor.

The free flow of credit is a constant incentive to economic growth. Timber on a slope, oil and minerals in the earth, arable land or food in the sea mean nothing until man converts them into items of shelter, food, power and transport. The activating influence on our raw materials comes from the mind in action, which is *management*, and from money in movement, which is *credit*, the catalyst of trade.

Credit gives us power to act or transfer action, and like all power, it requires direction and control. Credit is granted on the quality of the risk, and the more light shed on the risk the easier the decision to accept. No man likes to step into the dark.

Credit illuminates the trade lanes of land, air and sea, and is the most dynamic symbol of the world of free enterprise.

Risk In Decision Making

History repeats itself with some interesting variations, and the variations are enough to make prophecy hazardous. The rise and fall of kingdoms had common—but never identical—causes. The shifting trends of our economy, ranging from boom to bust, with all the stages of prosperity and recession in between, have similar characteristics, but their components are never the same.

Perhaps that's the way it should be. The margin for error is what makes life and business attractive to managers, investors, and even customers who share in the risk. The margin for error can never be wholly eliminated. When a decision is made, management is risking its judgement against intangibles which can neither be controlled nor foreseen.

It's a good manager who prepares for contingencies, but doesn't ask for complete insurance against disaster. He uses every known device to detect danger. Yet when the time comes, he accepts the calculated risk with all the confidence of a trained gymnast timing his leap from ring to ring. No progress is made without decisions involving a variety of hazards.

Decisions are made up of facts, vision, and guts—and the third is the most necessary element when the going gets rough. In the race for profits, there are no handicaps for the inept or the weary.

The slow runners in any industry usually reflect slow decisions or no decisions at a time when management faces risks. These are the companies whose future is constantly imperilled by new products, new methods, and new markets. They suffer competitively from obsolescent machinery; boxed-in, antiquated factories; dislocated markets; excessive, costly, depreciating stock, sluggish, second-rate outlets, and unimaginative advertising and sales promotion.

The decision to avoid decisions is the worst decision of all. Not all the computers in creation can compensate for the timid management that avoids the challenges of the daily market place and tries to play it safe. No matter how efficient a management may be with electronic brains to guide its judgement, there comes a time when it must face the mental wrestling match on its own. Then, if it is worthy of its responsibilities, it will say " Now " —and make the courageous decision.

Leader And Follower

No thinking man gives blind allegiance to a point of view because of his faith in a leader. And no man's business judgement can be immune to the influence of forces, generated in other areas of life, which impinge on the channels of industry and trade. There are tidal influences in mass thinking, and there are shifting currents in social attitudes. Every political, educational, and economic shift bears directly upon the profits of risk-takers in business, the income of professional men, and the wages of workers.

In the reckoning of the professional politician, the tidal impact of trends overwhelms the independent and contrary minor currents of thinking individuals. History supports the public leader's reliance on group psychology, yet there is increasing evidence of the influence wielded by the individual who refuses to be labelled and taken for granted. Group loyalty without intellectual appraisal of the merits of a cause is another name for bulk stupidity. Herein lies the greatest challenge of democracy: intelligent minority action can be impeded by majority inertia. This is true of the action of any splinter group, left or right.

The black-and-white label of reactionary on any political, social, or economic question is likely to be in error. A statistical average is helpful in dealing with £s or products, but it seldom gives an accurate picture of the individual mind. There are times when the typical citizen surrenders part of his personality to a group cause, but he rarely wears an indelible stamp of affiliation. The unions have never been able to deliver " a solid vote " to a political candidate. The farm bloc cannot claim all the men who till the soil, nor can the Chambers of Commerce speak for every business man.

Britain has no want of aspirants to leadership. But, to qualify, they must give evidence of an understanding of the total economy and society. The citizen looking for guidance should not give his support to any individual whose motives, integrity, and capacity for leadership are untested.

Every generation has its quotas of heroes, martyrs, and demagogues whose urge for the spotlight is rarely satisfied. Men of honourable, as well as men of ignoble, designs share hunger for acclaim, and the good leader's right to applause and recognition should not be denied. Sometimes it is the only tangible benefit he gets for a life of dedication to a fickle public. The next best thing to a good leader is a discerning follower who understands the man he is following, knows where he is going and the reasons for taking that road.

Unemployment Compensation

Part of the cost of doing business is the taxes we pay, and part of those taxes is used to help people in financial trouble in times of economic change. Unemployment Compensation, one of the most important forms of this help, is a programme conceived in good faith and generally well administered. Yet it invites an economic evil that is growing in many communities.

One of the most helpful persons in the village or small town used to be the " odd job man ", who could repair a pathway, paint a small building, mend a fence and take on a multitude of other odd jobs. He worked by the hour, day or week, unhampered by the complications of the rules that now regulate temporary employment. Maybe the " odd job man " is still around, but he is no longer available for spring or autumn jobs when the house needs attention, or the garden could do with a clean up. He is collecting unemployment pay. He can't take the risk of making a few pounds and losing those payments. In his case, certainly, unemployment pay increases unemployment by deferring initiative.

Inflation And Its Illusion

When you expand a zero, you still have nothing. That's about all inflation can promise us in the long run. We can see this if we distinguish between the justifiable price we pay for the increased benefits of better living and the mathematical deception by which prosperity is magnified and distorted. There have been material gains in the form of shelter, food, travel, education, and recreation, and there has been a net gain in per capita wealth to pay the price. When a person gives more in effort to get more in equity, there is no inflation. But any attempt to evade the effort or reduce our own moral physical contribution to the system that supports us is inflationary, because it means we are demanding more for thinking less and doing less.

The danger is not in a better level of living but in our willingness to take something for nothing and expect a net gain.

Inflation is not primarily a matter of money but of social behaviour. Currency values are a statistical guide established for the convenience of traders of goods and services. Long ago, Bishop Fleetwood, a cleric with an eye for economics, studied " prices current " from the Battle of Hastings in 1066 to the year 1707. He found that barter, a clumsy method of exchange, was a fair test of values. For instance, the price of a pair of shoes at any period was equal to a day's labour in the fields or at the work bench. Even today, the price of shoes on a barter basis is still about a day's effort for a working man.

Inflation must be defined according to its rate of escalation, beginning with the " creeping " variety, which is usually calculated at one to two per cent per year, and accelerating to the " runaway " pace which has destroyed the economy of many nations. A postage stamp paid off a mortgage after the collapse of the German mark, following World War I. Prior to the Communist takeover in China, the silver foil covering the paper yuan was worth more than the money it covered.

The tough elastic skin of our economy can stand the moderate pressures of economic expansion. Indeed, a shockingly high percentage of businessmen—particularly retailers—feel that moderate inflation is desirable. They reason that it reduces sales resistance, increases gross profit, helps repay heavy indebtedness and speeds up the collection of money owing. A creeping inflation offers them a kind of false security.

Some economists defend a creeping inflation as the necessary price we pay for accelerating the momentum of trade. They welcome the Keynesian philosophy of spending our way to prosperity.

All this is a way of " cashing in on a good thing." It is an illusion of progress. Inflation is a lazy cover-up for lack of business energy and ingenuity, mediocre sales promotion and wishful thinking. When momentum takes the place of management direction, a day of reckoning is inevitable. Deflation, when it comes, is as impartial as a bomb thrown in a crowd. It leaves many economic scars on the body of business.

What should be the counterattack to inflationary forces?

One way to slow up inflation is to fight it with a vigourous programme of management economy and productivity that stabilizes wages and prices. Any sudden drop in prices is a painful jolt, but a pause on the long-term price escalator would be welcome in many industries. Even a slight decline achieved by better techniques, better management, better selling, and less featherbedding could recover lost markets.

Whenever the business cycle takes a dip, the same hard lesson is repeated. Good management meets the challenges of falling sales volume. It finds a way to cut costs and weeds out the dead wood. Manufacturers who are determined to succeed replace inefficient machinery. Retailers clean out their sluggish stocks, restudy the market and put some zip into the sales people behind the counter.

But the alert manager does not wait for a sales push from an inflationary wind. He knows that inflation is a subtle, habit-forming drug that must be resisted by heroic self-discipline. He knows that the businessman who welcomes inflation is taking a thief into partnership.

The Challenge Of Automation

In generations past, frightened weavers destroyed Watt's steam-driven looms, hand compositors tried to wreck the Morgenthaler linotype, and farmers refused to turn the loam with Charles Newbold's new iron plough because they feared it would poison the soil.

Despite all our progress, ignorance and fear are still the enemy of the machine, particularly where both are rooted in the concept of automation. But today the relative benefits, promises and forebodings of automation are more exciting and disturbing to spectators than to participants, for this is a game in which fewer and fewer people make more and more goods. Prophets with funereal faces and lugubrious tones warn that the moment we achieve the ultimate in automated production, the consumer will disappear with the worker. We have heard that threat since Watt's first steam weaving frame was smashed by handicraftsmen. In Watt's time it took one family on the farm to produce food for one family in industry. Today one man on a farm can feed almost a hundred at the lathe. The number of miners diminishes as the volume increases, despite fewer hours.

To what extent does the productive capacity of the machine exceed the upward curve of consumption? Is there an answer to the apparent contradiction of poverty in paradise? Can the population explosion provide consumers who can pay for what they eat, wear and waste in an economy that must support unemployables who need to be fed, clothed, educated and amused in idleness?

Before we acknowledge the prospect of economic paraylsis, we must ask the cost accountant, the engineer in research and development and the marketer to appraise the situation with long, co-operative looks. We must also give more attention to two key people in this dilemma, the man who sells and the man who buys, and find a way of bringing them together with less fumbling.

The modern salesman has many tools, some old and many new. There is no tool more effective than market research. Every product and service requires different handling, and smart sales management turns floodlights on the market place.

The automated fact-finder can be the servant of the salesman by pinpointing data on customer desires. Stocks can be moved on a computerized schedule to 50 million people. Before we accept the dismal prospect of social defeat in an hour of mechanical triumph, we ought to test our resources as thinkers and doers in stimulating the demand-supply relationship with intelligently directed sales promotion and more face-to-face selling.

A lot of people will require a lot of things for a long time before the machine catches up with consumer needs. Nor can the producer of consumer goods employ impersonal devices to displace the personal appeal and value of the salesman. There is a need for the human touch, no matter how well the inanimate thing is designed, costumed and manipulated.

Too much attention is given to the Dismal Jimmy auguries of those who never sold a thing or risked a penny on a new product, while not enough co-ordinating support is offered the marketer and salesman, who are expected to move merchandize and perform the necessary services. The inordinate drive towards volume without equivalent effort towards excellence should worry the makers and distributors of merchandize more than the wailing of pessimists. Let's try more science in selling, but let's also put more motivation into individual sales techniques before we call automation a thing of good or evil. It is a mixed blessing perhaps, but let's find out what's good about it first.

Decentralization

The traffic manager complains that he can't get the ear of top management. So does the office manager. So does the plant engineer. All encounter deliberate road blocks at upper levels of management authority.

If the managing director surounds himself with a palace guard whose duty is to fend off inquiry and smother suggestions with a smile, then middle management can only wander back to the desk frustrated. But if the men around him have a topside view of responsibility and are eager to overcome problems quickly without a loss in executive morale, they will know when to assume the burden and when to step aside.

Supervisory management should be trained to make decisions. When middle management is given enough liberty of action, it acquires mental and moral strength to meet situations and make decisions. Beyond these areas, top management must be informed and must define its purpose and scope.

When top management limits authority and penalizes the adventurous, then it invites slow rust. Acting on its own initiative, middle management will make mistakes, but the more it acts, the fewer the mistakes will be. It might even reach the point of making decisions on subjects where the top brass never had the information, foresight, or courage to take action. When top management hamstrings middle management because of its own vanity or insecurity, then the business becomes a victim of mental mildew. Mistakes are the price of progress.

The best way to handle middle management is to give executives on their way up a chance to find their own answers and be responsible for them. Why step on their fingers? The risk is small compared to the results to be achieved.

Obsolescence —Men And Machines

In the competitive world of industry, one can't be philosophical or complacent about operating an obsolescent machine. The path of progress and profits is marked by the junk yards of earlier decades. It takes courage as well as capital to install new machinery.

But the problem of keeping ahead of invention and refinement in industry is not half so serious with machines as with men. A good machine may last for years. Circumstances can occasionally justify its existence, even if it is not as efficient as the latest model. A good mind, however, may deteriorate rapidly if, in complacency or lethargy, it ignores the daily setting-up exercises of ideas.

If industrial design isn't permanent, neither are the habits, whims, or desires of the public that influence the shape, size and function of the product. Change in industry turns raw material stock piles into riches or rubbish, and machinery into capital assets or junk.

Obsolescence begins first in the mind that prefers reminiscence to planning. It takes root in mental habits long before it spreads its cobwebs over machinery. If management stays young and alert in its thinking, obsolescence is seldom included among its negative assets.

99

Image

Currently, the word " image " is in vogue, and businessmen rush to the mirror to see what kind of an impression
they are making on the public. Sometimes they are more
concerned with the image than the fact.

The Greek dramatists used masks to portray moods
—fixed images of grief, joy, envy, anger, or other emotions they wished to convey to an audience. It was a
synthetic device to convey an emotional setting for a
comic or tragic situation. But in our day, a corporate
mask conceals little when a company faces its employees,
shareholders, or the public. Our motives, sincere or
otherwise, are somehow transparent and no illusion of
word or symbol can disguise them.

Public-relations advisors will advise management on
the good image that can be created in community relations by a progressive, co-operative attitude on such
issues as housing, smoke abatement, water supply, or
the bad image created by ugly buildings, labour disputes,
or tax protests. But what about the faceless image
created by the less-than-candid behaviour of management whose motives and policies are concealed in
silence?

Children make faces in the mirror and sometimes

frighten themselves in the process. When a business gets self-conscious about the face it is making before customers, employees, and shareholders, it might be wise to stop playing make-believe and try being natural, with all the warts and beauty spots visible. The personality of a business is reflected in the lives of the people it influences, as well as in the attitude of its management and the nature and quality of its product.

When a company " loses face " because of poor labour policies or shoddy products and services, no mask is going to cover up its guilt or folly. The face that a company creates is reflected in the eyes of the consumer who appraises the product or service. He looks at the translucent facade of management and sees the conscience at work, for no mask can conceal the intention of its wearer.

Strenuous efforts at image-making stem from the attempt to refute the traditional charges against the capitalistic system and its company offspring. It is often an attempt to make amends for the major sins of an earlier generation, or for lesser sins of the present one. *But if we keep the company face clean, we will have little need for cosmetics.* Enlightened management prefers to scrub with plain soap and water.

What Is A Fair Profit?

Only your customer and competitor can help you answer that question with assurance. The government may try by tax rates to fix a profit ceiling, and critics who never risked capital for gain may devise their own restraints on the profit motive. In truth, a fair profit is the mechanism by which risk is rewarded and survival assured in the market place.

The term profiteer was created in World War I, but it had its antecedents centuries earlier in the never-ending wrangles of Europe. When goods are in short supply the privateers of industry move in, and there is no better invitation than the critical needs of war emergency.

If profits are necessary in a war economy, they are even more justified in the armed truce economy in which we exist today.

Shareholders toss no bouquets at managers when dividends are omitted. Employees get no raises or profit participation when losses are greater than gains. Union leaders have no respect for the manager who does not show a profit under competitive pressure. Profit is an incentive for growth and a fair profit is all that your customers and competitors allow you to earn under usual market conditions.

102

The profit motive is ingrained in the spirit of man. It is expressed succinctly in the biblical parable of talents. In it, the servants of the king who invested their talents (units of gold) and showed a profit on their investment were rewarded by the king for their sense of risk. Only the servant who buried his talent in fear of loss was reprimanded. His risk capital was assigned to a successful manager.

The objective of any business is to render a service to a customer and a community. The means to that end is a profit margin that insures the continuity of the business and the proper reward to the shareholders through dividends, to the employees through wages, and to the nation through taxes. The public servants who are paid out of tax revenues have no affection for the profitless operation. National defence, public education, social institutions and other services rendered to the citizen are the direct or indirect result of the profitability of business ventures.

Community Initiative

Is it necessary for the Government to maintain a blood bank for periodic transfusions to the body economic? Or does the shot in the arm weaken industry's capacity for meeting the uncertainties of free enterprise? To what degree should business be spoon-fed with incentives?

Progress is a disruptive agent. Pain and profit go together in the dislocation of manufacturing and distribution, and the more change, the more scar tissue. Can we hope to maintain prosperity with an even pulse as modern research introduces new materials into manufacturing and mass marketing jars production schedules?

It is folly to expect a windfall in tax benefits to take up the slack in management talent, sales initiative or product research. It is easy to mistake inflation for growth. The price of prosperity is mental and physical sweat: the energy of ideas put to work in the creative design of useful goods and services. There is no easy road to profits.

Economic tools are not designed to take the place of individual enterprise. The man who leans too hard on a statistical prop is likely to fall on his face. The index components of prosperity do not move at the same velocity. Sales and stock have a different rhythm, with sales jerky as a hare and stock heavy-footed as an elephant,

104

but this historical difference is lessening as the computer makes stock control more sensitive to demand.

Government advisors attempt to measure the pace of economic growth in percentage points, but the whims of the consumer is still the unstable element in the formula for progress. What motivates the consumer to spend one year and save the next is as much a problem of psychology as of economics. But *what makes a business successful*, regardless of tax incentives and statistical guidelines, *is the management drive* of the individuals who generate their own power without waiting for an external push.

The business community welcomes vision and understanding in its relationship with government. There is no such thing as " free " enterprise for industry and trade, but management must have freedom of action within the length of the legal leash, and that limited freedom includes the right to make some mistakes and pay for them out of invested capital. The growth and profit factors in business cannot be controlled or assured by tax palliatives or by any other carrot on the stick. Prosperity is best achieved when men must fight in open competition, according to the rules of the game.

Stock Exchange And High Street

In our industrial and distributive system The Stock Exchange is the means and The High Street the end, and neither can exist without the other. The Stock Market stands for the risk capital which keeps the gears turning throughout the Country. The tempo of the cash register's jingle in the High Street influences the chattering stock market ticker tape.

Credit travels almost with the speed of light from bankers, insurance companies, and suppliers, giving support to thousands of enterprises throughout Britain. There is a constant return of invested savings flowing into the Stock Market and back into the channels of industry and trade. The thrifty pound, the investment pound, and the credit pound chase each other in a time cycle that provides facilities and services for our people.

The stock exchange is more than a convenience for traders in securities. It is a catalyst for the swift conversion of goods and services into cash and credit, and it works to the advantage of buyer and seller alike. The stock exchange, and Commodity Markets are a storage house of power for our commercial life. All these arenas of business action deal in " futures " and reflect tomorrow's progress.

Just as the stereotyped image of big business as the foe of small business fades with a close-up look, so the ogre of the speculative Stock Exchange melts in the light of appraisal. The Stock Market is a device for energizing business, and such an instrument is no better than the behaviour of the men at the controls. The Stock Market is the servant of the High Street. Usually it serves it well. But the servant betrays the master when the gamble becomes more attractive than the moderate risk. It is readily apparent, however, that the Market Investor and the High Street Manufacturer and Merchant have one dominant interest in common: the profitable management of business.

Trade, Understanding And Peace

Man in his hour of greatest achievement is also in his day of greatest anxiety. In this, our generation, he has broken through many barriers in the natural order. His feats have dwarfed the wonders of Merlin, Aladdin, and Jonah.

He has mastered many enigmas in nature. He outflies the condor, outdives the whale, outspeeds sound, and requires new concepts of measurement in time and space as he creates the infinitesimal and the gargantuan. He has poked holes in the sky, sifted stardust, walked the moon, and touched sea bottom at its greatest depth.

What is there left for him to conquer? Just one thing: himself. He is still confused about his identity and his ultimate destiny but tomorrow approaches and he has to do something about it. He is faced with a paradox: Although he can't get along with his neighbour, he can't get along without him either. There can be no dispute about his need for survival as a member of society in which personal freedom and enterprise make concessions for the common good of neighbours and nations.

Is man his brother's keeper? We have the depressing symbol of Cain and Abel, the hopeful symbol of Joseph and his brothers, the inspiring symbol of Damon and

Pythias. In his social intercourse, man has exchanged cultural assets, political ideas, ethical and religious concepts. In business intercourse, man demonstrates a propensity to give and take as a means of fair exchange of goods and services.

Trade as a social instrument for better understanding has been tested for centuries against the difficulties of language, custom, and distance, and the barriers of tariffs, embargoes, and piracy. As international commerce is encouraged or restricted for political and diplomatic reasons, the social influence of the creation, processing, and exchange of products takes on increased significance.

Any handicap to the free flow of goods and services weakens one of the most valuable and desirable supports to the peace of nations. The exchange of material benefits sets the pace for the exchange of the higher, if less tangible, spiritual and cultural values which identify the civilized man. Trade is a willing servant to the loftier aspirations of man. It demonstrates the rational benefits of a long-term mutual respect of rights and privileges.

Trade can help man to conquer himself. All physical conquests are of secondary importance unless human values have priority. In trade, man shows a net gain as a thinking creature with a sense of responsibility to his fellow man. When there is a constant exchange of goods, services, and credits, there is always hope for progress towards understanding.

Consumer Behaviour

The average consumer measures wealth in terms of utility and is more than willing to spend it on service and recreation for his family—on cars, appliances, home improvements, clothing, books, entertainment, and travel. The fact that he takes as lively an interest in saving as in spending only proves that to him money is a means to an end, not a miserly objective in itself. He is not impelled by fear of tomorrow, nor is he doing without essentials for the sake of building up his bank statement. He is under no obligation to clutter up his garage, kitchen, or living room with anything more than what he wants. When the consumer shows reluctance to spend, he is often serving industry's future needs by creating a thrift backlog of risk capital.

The customer will continue to indulge his whims at the market place, eager one day and stubborn the next. And the great game of wits will go on, for the individual is still elusive enough in his buying habits to defeat any smug formula that would predict his behaviour.

That's what makes the game fascinating. We might imagine that we would like nothing better than " easy picking " from the buyer's open palm, but there wouldn't be any competitive fun in it for us.

PART VI

Communication

Dramatize The Message

The power of suggestion has both good and evil aspects. Someone hijacks a passenger plane, and a half-dozen idiots follow suit. A sneak on a rooftop hurls a brick at a policeman, and a dozen morons pull bricks from chimneys and endanger passersby. A vandal breaks a window at one school, and soon the authorities have to put a glazier on the job at a dozen others. In one generation, the power of suggestion sets students swallowing live goldfish; in the next, it has them growing beards.

Despite centuries of civil discipline, virtue and order hold only a narrow margin of control over the brute in man. That is why the shrewd demagogue, with his ability to spread a contagious mood, is a continuing menace.

But eloquence and showmanship are not limited to the provocateur or evangelist. Sane leadership in science, religion or business can dramatize its message and merits through a contagion of spirit.

Human nature suffers from emotional hunger, and the forces of progress and growth in society should know how to satisfy that hunger with a skill equal to that of the knave and charlatan.

The Most Explosive Thing
In The World

Alfred Nobel, founder of the Peace Prize, was born in Stockholm in 1833. As a young man he perfected a commercial explosive, which he called dynamite. It has served industry well, ripping apart the bowels of mountains to loosen veins of iron ore, prying free coal deposits wedged in seams of slate, and pulling down hillsides rich in copper, silver and many rarer metals. It has dug ditches to drain swamps and salvage drowned acres and cleared trees for farmland and roadways. Nobel designed dynamite for man's welfare—not his destruction. As evidence of his ethical and moral intentions, he used his profits to establish the Peace Prize.

The atom-splitters, from Einstein and Fermi to the men who made the instrument that obliterated much of Hiroshima and Nagasaki, prefer to think of the atomic pile as generating power for merchants ships and power plants.

The Chinese invented gunpowder for their ceremonial firecrackers many centuries before the Italian states employed explosives for their guns in the fourteenth century. Over the years, the tools of war have become deadlier. Now, for better or for worse, we have dynamite, TNT, cordite, nuclear fission, and nuclear fusion. What

H

then is the most explosive thing in the world?

Actually, it is none of these. The most explosive thing in the world today is printer's ink. Why? Because it can detonate ideas that will move the minds of men with a force infinitely greater and more lasting than the whirlwind loosed by splitting an atom. Printer's ink serves good or evil, but the evidence on the positive side far outweighs the negative. For when a man with a vision of man's higher destiny touches ink to paper, its blackness holds the light to the world.

In his urge to make the inherent power of printer's ink the servant of the arts and sciences, Nobel offered annual rewards to the talented writers who used the printed word for the aesthetic pleasure of their fellow men. Many have left a deep impression on the minds and souls of men.

Judgement of the printed word comes not through repression but through exposure, and its power as a force for good depends upon the discipline of the emotional by the rational. Though atomic power may threaten man's destruction, printer's ink holds promise of his salvation. Personally, we'll take our chances on the superior force of printer's ink.

Management's Fight Against "Technophobia"

How can we combat the fear of automation now rampant in plant and office? Much of the fear, costly in both time and morale, would vanish if top management paid as much attention to psychology as it does to technology.

The acceptance of change is primarily a problem in communication. If employees—manager and worker alike—were told what is coming, when it is coming, and how it will affect them, half the resentment and anxiety could be eliminated.

The opposition to technological innovation is seldom rational. The negative reaction is not so much resistance to progress as to actions which challenge ego or status.

Progress is a pulsating spiral, expanding and contracting under the pressure of new ideas, new resources, new techniques. Technology today affects at least ten aspects of our commercial and social existence. The net gain realized in the past decade has been enormous, but it has created a difficulty for almost every benefit—obstacles that in many instances could have been removed by foresight, by not taking too much for granted, by good communication, and plain understanding of basic human emotions.

In each of the following areas influenced by the technological revolution, the obvious remedy is a planned programme of information across the board to share-holders, officers, employees, unions, customers, suppliers and the public.

Top management in an old establishment, especially a family-owned enterprise, is often reluctant to accept a change affecting product, methods, or markets. Yet few companies in business today makes the same product for the same market in the same way it did ten years ago. During a recent recession, *Dun's Review* asked a cross section of manufacturers what they planned to do about obsolescent equipment. Many stated they would have to have new machine tools as an aid in lowering costs and meeting competition, but they mentioned the lack of capital as a major difficulty. Those whose companies were closely held or family-owned stated their reluctance to accept a broader base of public ownership. It is in this very category, however, that many of the shotgun and tax-haven mergers frequently occur.

Actually, it was more obsolescence of management than machinery that led to absorption and oblivion for family enterprises with a three- or four-generation her-aldry. Alert management in any medium-sized firm needs only to follow the research and development patterns of larger corporations, which often find it pro-fitable to sacrifice basic patent protection and share the benefits of new materials and techniques. Magazines pro-vide current data, designs, and case histories on money-making ideas, free for the asking. But the eyes and the ears of management must be alert to what is going on. And management must inform all its executives and managers when the decision to launch a new programme has been made. Secrecy is no balm to the ego of men left " out in the cold."

Money talks, and no R & D project can move ahead

on a rational basis without a definition of the objective, some indication of the cost of achieving it, and a reasonable understanding of how much and what type of financing is required. Since the odds are against a new product, these costs must include the expense of market research to test consumer acceptance, retailer co-operation, and the attainable profit margin, as well as all the costs from design to point-of-sale promotion. The budget for any idea should also include enough money to pay for one serious mistake.

Research must have freedom of action. It must be responsible to top management for its direction. Years of fact-finding effort can be wasted when there are intermediaries with the power to intervene, to pigeonhole, or to thwart the results. The technological revolution of this century began in the laboratory, which should never be a barn for sacred cows. Both scientists and psychologists require independence in their work.

When the results of research are thrust upon a departmental executive who is unaware of company plans and policy, he is apt to offer a shrug of the shoulders or a snide comment instead of a word of enthusiasm. The communications effort should first be directed to the middle-management executives who must interpret the wishes of top management.

There was a time when the office manager was the official whipping boy, the man who would do what he was told, take the blame for managment errors, and perform a thousand and one assignments. Most larger companies—where office management was once considered a maintenance expense, the first to suffer under crash decisions of economy—have today made amends. One company with many branch offices called its managers to head office for a month's retraining, converting fear into confidence with a few days of intensive instruction on the

117

function of new equipment. Top management is beginning to learn that its estimate of middle-management activities has been foggy, and its attitude towards loyal and sometimes bewildered people, crass and cruel.

In a family company, the office has too often been the haven for executive misfits, for "island emperors," lording it over clerks performing meaningless and obsolete functions. It has also been the place where talent is permitted to rust and expenses are encouraged to mount.

To some degree, the sales department has suffered from singular neglect, especially when new products replace the old. Attention is given to the effectiveness of the commissioned sales staff, but the salaried house salesman, often a mediocre performer, is permitted to starve on husks of old catalogues. Yet upgrading run-of-the-mill salesmen is a necessity when new products are introduced. It requires intensive retraining with sales engineering guidance. Most of all, the entire sales staff needs advance information from the top to eliminate speculative gossip with customers about product shifts and service procedures.

Technology upsets production routines with its improvements and affects the mental attitude of the man at the lathe, loom, or press. This is a most sensitive spot in industrial relations, especially when mechanization, automation, or a change in the product means a shift in jobs and skills, and perhaps a temporary dip in take-home pay. Unless the worker is informed promptly and candidly, he will believe the worst of the washroom gossip.

Management and labour unions have an equal responsibility to advise skilled workers of the reasons for job changes and the necessity for retraining. A skilled riveter may resent being trained as an apprentice welder, but once he knows the inevitability of change, he will

118

alter his attitude from resentment to co-operation. The same is true of the white-collar employee, as data processing equipment and office mechanization change his routines. Creatures of habit must be re-oriented to their different surroundings, yet the task isn't too difficult if they know the benefits.

In this generation of plant management, there is a new man of action—the systems specialist—who frequently gets in the hair of the factory engineer or the executive in charge. The duel of wits is a variant of a continuing staff and management wrangle, in which vanity, prestige, and self-justification are involved. When the systems man is aggressive, and the executive is insecure, there is bound to be conflict, much of it unnecessary, costly, and disturbing to company morale. The irritant could be removed if both parties were brought together at the earliest stage of the new programme. Here is where top management needs a lesson in basic psychology, especially an understanding of the factors which motivate men to accept or reject ideas.

Any unexplained situation can set a rumour buzzing in the factory. For instance, when a public-relations executive escorted a group of visiting Belgian businessmen through one factory, as part of a good-will programme, the rumour started that the factory was moving to the continent as part of a cost-saving programme. Again, a photograph of a new power punch, taken at the request of the supplier who needed an action shot for an advertisement, led a shop steward to tell the union that a time study for piecework was under way.

A notice on the bulletin board or a statement to the foreman would have prevented these seeds of discontent and anxiety from scattering about the premises. Industrial relations are improved when union officials are called in and given candid information on expected changes in product, production methods or work rules.

Technology will influence customer relationships, and the changeover of product or method cannot be taken casually. Planning, design, engineering, sales, and promotion expense are all at stake when the customer makes his decision. If he has used a product for a period of time, he may resist the change in format or design—or he may welcome the new look.

Engineering improvements may create a profit potential in reduced costs, but will the customer accept them? These changes may require the re-education of customers as to the use of the product, education which includes details about inspection, packaging, deliveries, and guarantees.

Often, regular, trusted suppliers suffer when new materials are introduced. Many maintain stocks of semi-processed goods and special tools. They have a right to information, for better or for worse, and should not be " left holding the baby " when an early word could save them needless loss of money. The new supplier must have his way smoothed for him, too. He cannot be expected to understand the habits, foibles, and routines of a company overnight. There must be a period of acclimatization in which he can learn plant procedures, purchasing and accounting methods, and other patterns of company activity and policy.

The public in general—as distinct from the customer in particular—should be informed about significant changes in product or service. The public mind absorbs impressions, some of them slightly out of focus, and its opinion of a company can be the result of a minor neglect or trivial courtesy. The way to the public is through newspapers, magazines, radio, TV, and direct mail. The public should be informed of such matters as proposed factory location shifts, new factory acquisitions, and new products to be advertised and distributed. The public includes shareholders, who shouldn't have to wait for the annual report to get the news.

Where technology has an aspect of scientific glamour, there is an audience among teachers and students. Many leading companies are creating educational material for schools and colleges.

We cannot run too far ahead of current acceptance of new tools and procedures. The pioneers in industry often go broke waiting for the parade to catch up. England had steam-driven omnibuses in 1810, but the vehicles were years ahead of pneumatic tyres and hard-surfaced highways. In the past, buyers of computers occasionally learned that they neither needed the computers nor understood how to use them. It took the buyers years of intellectual effort to learn to ask good questions and even longer to get usable answers and apply them to specific company problems.

The purchase of any automated machine must be justified by its profit potential—but above this consideration is the ethical and social challenge that arises when automation disturbs the social order.

Growth is often more painful than decay, and doubly so under the insistent pressures of technology. At no time should techniques take precedence over people. Workers have always feared the machine. And fear teams up with envy and jealousy when change endangers authority or prestige.

The answer to technophobia is candour. When the systems men, management consultants, and industrial engineers wander through the plant or office, they should be advertised in advance and carefully introduced to executives, supervisors, and foremen in their true role as fact-finders. Their forerunner, the efficiency expert, got a reputation as an industrial spy largely because of his furtive attitude in making notes and his air of immunity.

There is no need for such melodramatics today. Honesty and consideration will pave the way for changes that are essential in our changing world. The first step in that direction is an adequate communications programme.

A Common Language

When we say of a man, "He doesn't speak our language," what do we mean? This familiar statement, heard often in business discussions, has many shades of meaning. It implies that lack of understanding is a problem of definition and of ethics.

Precise meaning is as important in business as in diplomacy, both of which are afflicted with the vagueness of doubletalk. Since we use words to communicate, a common vocabulary for the exchange of ideas, opinions, and values is necessary.

Perhaps the hub of the problem is the "will to be understood." Where this desire exists, doubts can be resolved in candour without resort to jargon. Where this desire is lacking, communication falters. No words have ever been devised that will make men honest if their motives are not honest. Contracts between management and labour, vendor and supplier depend on mutual acceptance and good faith. Written words may clarify obligations, but they cannot enforce them unless promise and performance are welded by sincerity of intent.

Trade is occasionally more successful than diplomacy in finding a common ground for agreement. Many people of Central Africa speak Swahili, a tongue of

Bantu and Arabic origin that aids the business intercourse of more than a dozen countries from Ghana to Ethiopia. Cantonese, a mongrel Chinese tongue, borrows freely from Portuguese and English to serve the coastal trade of China. Pidgin English, a species of basic English that is devoid of grammar but embellished by inflection and gesture, is a recognized, well-used instrument of commerce in the harbours and the bazaars of the Indies.

A common language is not so important as the common need for fair exchange. Any man can speak " the other fellow's language," if he means what he says and backs up his words with action. Whether in business conversation, advertising, guarantees, or industrial activities, words and behaviour determine the image by which the individual or the company is judged. The man who is as good as his word speaks every man's language, because his will to be understood is apparent in every sentence he utters and every promise he makes.

What Is Publication?

Now that publishing houses are merging with television chains, and the impulse of the printed and spoken word takes on electronic power, the question of compatibility is asked. The first publisher was the tribal chieftain giving the law, and the second was the prophet or druid who communicated literature and created the myths which evolved into history. The first written communication was the caveman's pictographs which spiralled upward with the cuneiform characters on clay, to the block printed metaphoric symbols of the Chinese to the moveable type of Gutenberg in the fifteen century.

Publishing moved from the vocal to the visual with the printing press. The Hertzian wave and the DeForrest tube expanded the sensory range of publication from a few feet to a global reach, and with the satellite and all its accessories of communication, infinity is a reasonable target wherever there is " an eye to read or an ear to listen.'

The printed word is memory pattern for future reference. The libraries of the world are the memories of mankind as civilization evolved out of the haze of centuries. Now computer memory opens the door to an immesurable but easily accessible space area for cold storage reference and publication that can reduce the whole concept of accumulated wisdom, and secular revelation to a verbal key on a data processing tape.

The situation raises as many questions of ethical responsibilities as it does of techniques and application. How does creativity, copyright and liability fare in this indefinite region? At present we are not equipped with an imagination or sense of prophecy keen enough to chart a completely rational course. Only the empiric approach will determine and define both principle and policy. Utility must demonstrate the proper adjustment between competitive enterprise and the equities of the people and property involved. Looking back we observe how the " give and take " of the past century and a half in communication, automation and transportation has dovetailed common interests after years of painful tensions and concessions to the common good.

We live in an ultra-sensitive age in which physical dimensions of time and space have changed from hours to milli-seconds, and miles to instancy of touch, sight or hearing. The term " publication " takes on a much different glow as it rubs shoulders with " transistor tubes " than when it is applied to the linotype slug in its journey back and forth to the anonymity of the " melting-pot." However, the semantic quality of the " word " still generates the power which shapes opinion and decision no matter what form of publication it takes in the minds of men.

Instant Communication

Today, a bomb dropped on Haiphong echoes with a smashed window in an American library in Cairo, and a cry of protest from the left side of the House of Commons. Instant communication facilities, which connect the nervous system of humanity, can be what one man called " the gift of God in the hands of the Devil."

What can be done to give perspective as well as speed to communication? There is the danger of nuclear war in the electronic spark that sets the air waves in motion with inflammatory news. Science is servant to the highest bidder, good or evil. In this amoral circumstance, something must be done to maintain a favourable balance for men of goodwill who listen to reason.

The pulse of logic in human relations has a long wavelength, while the impulse of the passions of men listening to opportunists and demagogues is immediate. Yet in the long run, logic has prevailed with a slight margin over chauvinism and other aspects of a debauched national spirit. If national loyalties can be noble in purpose, the same impulses can be infected with political venom and misused in the name of democracy, freedom and other abstract terms of virtue. Evil does not care what flag it waves. Wars and most misunderstandings

127

at home and abroad are the result of bad definitions of peace, equity and justice.

The dangers that arise with the impact of instant communication cannot be erased by a return to an earlier era. But there is obvious peril in the emotional irritants of spot news. The news media must serve as responsible instruments of information. The earth is getting a bit too crowded for the spark to ignite the blood first and then—too late for preventive measures—the mind.